MEASURING INEQUALITY
TECHNIQUES FOR THE SOCIAL SCIENCES

F.A. Cowell
London School of Economics and Political Science

A HALSTED PRESS BOOK

John Wiley & Sons · New York

Published in the USA by

Halsted Press, a Division of
John Wiley & Sons Inc.
New York

330.0151
C 874 m

Library of Congress Cataloging in Publication Data

Cowell, Frank Alan
  Measuring inequality

  'A Halsted Press book'
  Bibliography: p.
  Includes index
  1. Income distribution.   2. Poverty.   I. Title.
HB601.C63   1977   330'.01'51   77-20851
ISBN 0-470-99349-9

Printed in Great Britain

Contents

Preface

'It is not the business of the botanist to
eradicate the weeds. Enough for him if he
can tell us just how fast they grow'.

- C. Northcote Parkinson,
Parkinson's Law.

The maligned botanist has a good deal to be said for him in
the company of a bunch of rival gardeners, each propagating
his own idea about the extent and the growth of thorns and
thistles in the herbaceous border, and each with a patent
weedkiller. I hope that this book will perform a similar
role in the social scientist's toolshed. It does not deal
with theories of the development of income distribution, of
the generation of inequality, or of other social weeds, nor
does it supply any social herbicides. However, it does give
a guide to some of the theoretical and practical problems
involved in an analysis of the extent of inequality thus
permitting an evaluation of the diverse approaches hitherto
adopted. In avoiding patent remedies for particular unwanted
growths, one finds useful analogies in various related
fields - for example, some techniques for measuring economic
inequality have important counterparts in sociological and
political studies. Thus, although I have written this as an

economist, I would like to think that students in these related disciplines will be interested in this material.

This book is deliberately limited in what it tries to do as far as expounding theory, examining empirical evidence, or reviewing the burgeoning literature is concerned. For this reason, a set of notes for each chapter is provided on pages 168 to 178. The idea is that if you have not already been put off the subject by the text, then you can follow up technical and esoteric points in these notes, and also find a guide to further reading. A full bibliography follows the notes. References to the bibliography (in either the main text or the notes) are made by citing the author, or the author and date. If more than one work in the same year is cited, these are distinguished by appending 'a', 'b' as appropriate; thus: von Obertrauser (1976a).

A satisfactory discussion of the techniques of inequality measurement inevitably involves the use of some mathematics. However, I hope that people who are allergic to symbols will nevertheless read on. If you are allergic, you may need to toil a little more heavily round the diagrams that are used fairly extensively in Chapters 2 and 3. In fact the most sophisticated piece of notation which it is essential that all should understand in order to read the main body of the text is the expression $\sum_{i=1}^{n} x_i$ representing the sum of n numbers indexed by the subscript i, thus: $x_1 + x_2 + x_3 + \ldots + x_n$. Also it is helpful if the reader understands differentiation, though this is not strictly essential. Those who are happy with mathematical notation may wish to refer directly to the appendix in which formal definitions are listed, and where proofs of some of the assertions in the text are given. The appendix also serves as a glossary of symbols used for inequality measures and other expressions.

I would like to thank Prof. M. Bronfenbrenner for the use of the table on page 101, and Dr. T. Stark and Prof. A.B. Atkinson for each allowing me to see in advance copies of forthcoming work. The number of colleagues and students who wilfully submitted themselves to reading drafts of this book was most gratifying. So I am very thankful for the comments of Tony Atkinson, Barbara Barker, John Bridge, David Collard, Shirley Dex, Les Fishman, Peter Hart, Kiyoshi Kuga, H.F. Lydall, M.D. McGrath, Neville Norman and Richard Ross; without them there would have been lots more mistakes. You, the reader, owe a special debt to Mike Harrison, John Proops and Mike Pullen who persistently made me make the text more intelligible. Finally, I am extremely grateful for the skill and patience of Sylvia Beech, Stephanie Cooper and Judy Gill, each of whom has had a hand in producing the text; 'so careful of the type she seems,' as Tennyson once put it.

The book is dedicated to my parents.

Frank A. Cowell
University of Keele
August 1977

1
First principles

'It is better to ask some of the questions
than to know all of the answers.'
                    - James Thurber (1945)
                    The Scotty Who Knew Too Much

'Inequality' is in itself an awkward word, as well as one
used in connection with a number of awkward social and
economic problems. The difficulty is that the word can
trigger quite a number of different ideas in the mind of a
reader or listener, depending on his training and
prejudices.

'Inequality' obviously suggests a departure from some
idea of equality. This may be nothing more than an unemotive
mathematical statement, in which case 'equality' just represents the fact that two or more given quantities are the
same size, and 'inequality' merely relates to differences
in these quantities. On the other hand, the term 'equality'
evidently has compelling social overtones as a standard
which it is presumably feasible for society to attain. The
meaning to be attached to this is not self-explanatory.
Indeed, Professors Rein and Miller recently interpreted
this standard of equality in nine separate ways - and the

1

list is probably not exhaustive:

One-hundred-percentism: in other words, complete horizontal equity - 'equal treatment of equals'.

The social minimum: here one aims to ensure that no one falls below some minimum standard of well-being.

Equalisation of lifetime income profiles: this focuses on inequality of future income prospects, rather than on the people's current position.

Mobility: that is, a desire to narrow the differentials and to reduce the barriers between occupational groups.

Economic inclusion: the objective is to reduce or eliminate the feeling of exclusion from society caused by differences in incomes or some other endowment.

Income shares: society aims to increase the share of national income (or some other 'cake') enjoyed by a relatively disadvantaged group - such as the lowest tenth of income recipients.

Lowering the ceiling: attention is directed towards limiting the share of the cake enjoyed by a relatively advantaged section of the population.

Avoidance of income and wealth crystallisation: this simply means eliminating the disproportionate advantages (or disadvantages) in education, political power, social acceptability and so on that may be entailed by an advantage (or disadvantage) in the income or wealth scale.

International yardsticks: a nation takes as its goal that it should be no more unequal than another 'comparable' nation.

Clearly, each of these criteria of 'equality' will influence in its own particular way the manner in which we define and measure inequality. And if I were to try to explore just these nine suggestions with the fullness that they deserve, I should easily make this book much longer than I wish. In order to avoid this mishap let us drastically reduce the problem by trying to set out what the essential ingredients of a Principle of Inequality Measurement should be. We shall find that these basic elements underlie a study of equality and inequality along almost any of the nine lines suggested above.

The ingredients are easily stated. For each ingredient

2

it is possible to use materials of high quality - with conceptual and empirical nuances finely graded. However, in order to make rapid progress, I have introduced some cheap substitutes which I have indicated in each case in the following list:

1. Specification of an individual social unit such as a single person, the nuclear family or the extended family. I shall refer casually to 'persons'.
2. Description of a particular attribute (or attributes) such as income, wealth, land-ownership or voting strength. I shall use the term 'income' as a loose coverall expression.
3. A method of representation and/or aggregation of the allocation of 'income' among the 'persons' in a given population.

The first ingredient is examined briefly as an issue of principle at the end of this chapter, and then reconsidered in terms of practical importance in Chapter 5. In Chapter 5 also we shall look at the second ingredient - again from the point of view of empirical requirements. The final ingredient will command much of our attention. We shall look at intuitive and formal methods of aggregation in Chapters 2 and 3; some of the basic issues are pursued in a later section of this chapter. However, it is to theoretical questions about the second ingredient that I now turn.

INEQUALITY OF WHAT?

In this section I want to explore some of the problems of the definition of a personal attribute, such as income, that is suitable for inequality measurement. This attribute can be interpreted in a wide sense if an overall indicator of social inequality is required, or in a narrow sense if one is concerned only with inequality in the distribution of some specific attribute or talent. Let us deal

first with the special questions raised by the former interpretation.

  If you want to take inequality in a global sense, then
it is evident that you will need a comprehensive concept of
'income' - an index that will serve to represent generally
a person's well-being in society. There are a number of
personal economic characteristics which spring to mind as
candidates for such an index - for example, wealth, lifetime income, or indeed income itself.

  While we might not go as far as Anatole France in describing wealth as a 'sacred thing', it has an obvious
attraction for us (as students of inequality). For wealth
represents a person's total immediate command over
resources. Hence, for each man or woman we have an aggregate which includes the money in the bank, the value of
holdings of stocks and bonds, the value of the house and
the car, his ox, his ass and everything that he has. There
are two difficulties with this. Firstly, how are these dis-
parate possessions to be valued and aggregated in money
terms? It is not clear that prices ruling in the market
(where such markets exist) appropriately reflect the
relative economic power inherent in these various assets.
Secondly, there are other, less tangible assets which
ought perhaps to be included in this notional command over
resources, but which a conventional valuation procedure
would omit. The major example of this is the presumed
prerogative of higher future incomes accruing to those
possessing greater education or training. Surely the value
of these income rights should be included in the calculation of a person's wealth just as is the value of other
income-yielding assets such as stocks or bonds? To do this
we need an aggregate of earnings over the entire life span.

4

Such an aggregate - 'lifetime income' - in conjunction
with other forms of wealth appears to yield the index of
personal well-being that we seek, in that it includes in a
comprehensive fashion the entire set of economic oppor-
tunities enjoyed by a person. The drawbacks, however, are
manifest. Since lifetime summation of *actual* income receipts
can only be performed once the income recipient is deceased
(which limits its operational usefulness), such a summation
must be carried out on *anticipated future* incomes. Following
this course we are led into the difficulty of forecasting
these income prospects and of placing on them a valuation
that appropriately allows for their uncertainty. Although
I do not wish to assert that the complex theoretical
problems associated with wealth and lifetime income are
insuperable, it is expedient to turn, with an eye on
Chapter 5 and practical matters, to income itself.

Income - defined as the increase in a person's command
over resources during a given time period - may seem restricted in comparison with the all-embracing nature of the
quantities discussed in the last paragraph. It has the
obvious disadvantages that it relates only to an arbitrary
time unit (such as one year) and thus that it excludes the
effect of past accumulations except in so far as these are
deployed in income-yielding assets. However, there are two
principal offsetting merits: (1) if income includes unearned income, capital gains and 'income in kind' as well
as earnings, then it can be claimed as a fairly comprehensive index of a person's well-being at a given moment;
(2) information on personal income is generally more widely
available and more readily interpretable than for wealth
or lifetime income.

Furthermore, note than none of the three concepts that

have been discussed cover the command over resources for
all goods and services in society. Measures of personal
wealth or income exclude 'social wage' elements such as the
benefits received from communally enjoyed items like
municipal parks, public libraries, the police, and ballistic
missile systems, the interpersonal distribution of which
services may only be conjectured.

In view of the difficulty inherent in finding a global
index of 'well-offness', we may prefer to consider the
narrow sense in which the problem of defining 'income' may
be taken. It can make sense to look at the inequality in
the endowment of some other personal attribute such as
consumption of a particular good, voting power, land
ownership, etc. This may be applied also to publicly owned
assets or publicly consumed commodities if we direct
attention not to *interpersonal* distribution but to *inter-
community* distribution - for example, the inequality in the
distribution of *per capita* energy consumption in different
countries. The problems concerning 'income' that I now
discuss apply with equal force to the wider interpretation
considered in the earlier paragraphs.

It is evident from the foregoing that two key characteristics of the 'income' index are that it be *measurable*
and that it be *comparable* among different persons. That
these two characteristics are mutually independent can be
demonstrated by two contrived examples. Firstly, to show
that an index might be measurable but not comparable,
take the case where well-being is measured by consumption
per head within families, the family rather than the
individual being taken as the basic social unit. Suppose
that consumption by each family in the population is known,
but that the number of persons is not. Then for each family,

6

welfare is measurable up to an arbitrary change in scale, in this sense: for family A doubling its income makes it twice as well off, trebling it makes it three times as well off; the same holds for family B; but A's welfare scale and B's welfare scale cannot be compared unless we know the numbers in each family. Secondly, to show that an index may be interpersonally comparable, but not measurable in the conventional sense, take the case where 'access to public services' is used as an indicator of welfare. Consider two public services, gas and electricity supply – households may be connected to one or to both or to neither of them, and the following scale (in descending order of amenity) is generally recognised:

    access to both gas and electricity
    access to electricity only
    access to gas only
    access to neither.

We can compare households' amenities – A and B are as well off if they are both connected only to electricity – but it makes no sense to say that A is *twice* as well off if he is connected to gas as well as electricity.

It is possible to make some progress in the study of inequality without measurability of the welfare index and sometimes even without full comparability. For most of the time, however,[†] I shall make both these assumptions, which may be unwarranted. For this implies that when I write the word 'income', I assume that it is so defined that adjustment has already been made for non-comparability on account of differing needs, and that fundamental differences in tastes (with regard to relative valuation of leisure and monetary income, for example) may be ruled out of

---

† I deal with certain cases of non-comparability in Chapter 5.

consideration.

The final point in connection with the 'income' index that I shall mention can be described as the 'constant amount of cake'.[†] We shall usually talk of inequality freely as though there is some fixed total of goodies to be shared among the population. This is definitionally true for certain quantities, such as the distribution of acres of land (except perhaps in the Netherlands). However, this is evidently questionable when talking about income as conventionally defined in economics. If an arbitrary change is envisaged in the distribution of income among persons, we may reasonably expect that the size of the cake to be divided - national income - might change as a result. Moreover if the size of the cake changes, either autonomously or as a result of some redistributive action, this change in itself may modify our view of the amount of inequality that there is in society. Having raised this important issue of the relationship between interpersonal distribution and the production of economic goods, I shall temporarily evade it by assuming that a given whole is to be shared as a number of equal or unequal parts. For some descriptions of inequality this assumption is irrelevant. However, since the size of the cake as well as its distribution is very important in social welfare theory, we shall consider the relationship between measured inequality and total income in the notes to Chapter 3, and examine the practical implications of a growing (or dwindling) cake in Chapter 5.

[†] 'Cake' is an odious cliché, but unfortunately there does not seem to be an alternative term of sufficient generality and simplicity.

INEQUALITY MEASUREMENT, JUSTICE AND POVERTY

So what is meant by an inequality measure? In order to introduce this device which serves as the third 'ingredient' mentioned previously, let us try a simple definition which roughly summarises the common usage of the term:

a scalar representation of the interpersonal differences in income within a given population.

Now let us take this bland statement apart.

1. The use of the word 'scalar' implies that all the different features of inequality are compressed into a single number - or a single point on a scale. Appealing arguments can be produced against the contraction of information involved in this aggregation procedure. Should we don this one-dimensional straightjacket when surely our brains are well-developed enough to cope with more than one number at a time? There are two points in reply here. Firstly, if we want a multi-number representation of inequality, we can easily arrange this by using a variety of indices each capturing a different characteristic of the social state, and each possessing attractive properties as a yardstick of inequality in its own right. Secondly, however, we often want to answer a question like 'has inequality increased or decreased?' with a straight 'yes' or 'no'. But if we make the concept of inequality multi-dimensional we greatly increase the possibility of coming up with ambiguous answers. For example, suppose we represent inequality by two numbers, each describing a different aspect of inequality of the same 'income' attribute. We may depict this as a point such as B in figure 1-1, which reveals that there is an amount I_1 of type 1 inequality, and I_2 of type 2 inequality. Obviously all points like C represent states of society that are more unequal than B

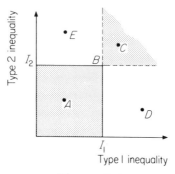

Figure 1-1

and points such as A represent less unequal states. But
it is much harder to compare B and D or to compare B and E.
If we attempt to resolve this difficulty, we will find
that we are effectively using a single-number representation of inequality after all.

2. What interpretation should be placed on the phrase
'numerical representation' in the definition? The answer to
this depends on whether we are interested in just the
ordering properties of an inequality measure or in the
actual size of the index and of changes in the index.

To see this, look at the following example. Imagine
four different social states A, B, C, D, and four rival
inequality measures I_1, I_2, I_3, I_4. The first column in
table 1-1 gives the values of the first measure, I_1,
realised in each of the four situations. Are any of the
other candidates equivalent to I_1? Notice that I_3 has a
strong claim in this regard. Not only does it rank A, B,
C, D in the same order, it also shows that the percentage
change in inequality in going from one state to another is
the same as if we use the I_1 scale. If this is true for all
social states, we will call I_1 and I_3 *cardinally equivalent*.
More formally, I_1 and I_3 are cardinally equivalent if one

Table 1-1

	I_1	I_2	I_3	I_4
A	.10	.13	.24	.12
B	.25	.26	.60	.16
C	.30	.34	.72	.20
D	.40	.10	.96	.22

scale can be obtained from the other by multiplying by a positive constant and adding or subtracting another constant. In the above case, we multiply I_1 by 2.4 and add on zero to get I_3. Now consider I_4: it ranks the four states A to D in the same *order* as I_1, but it does *not* give the same percentage differences (compare the gaps between A and B and between B and C). So I_1 and I_4 are certainly not cardinally equivalent. However, if it is true that I_1 and I_4 always rank any set of social states in the same order, we will say that the two scales are *ordinally equivalent.*[†] Obviously cardinal equivalence entails ordinal equivalence, but not vice versa. Finally we note that I_2 is not ordinally equivalent to the others, although for all we know it may be a perfectly sensible inequality measure.

Now let A be the year 1970, let B be 1960, and D be 1950. Given the question, 'Was inequality less in 1970 than it was in 1960?', I_1 produces the same answer as any other ordinally equivalent measure (such as I_3 or I_4): 'numerical representation' simply means a ranking. But, given the question, 'Did inequality fall more in the 1960s than it did in the 1950s?', I_1 only yields the same answer as other

---

† A mathematical note: I_1 and I_4 are ordinally equivalent if one may be written as a monotonically increasing function of the other, i.e. $I_1 = f(I_4)$, where $dI_1/dI_4 > 0$. An example of such a function is $\log(I)$.

cardinally equivalent measures (I_3 alone): inequality now
needs to have the same kind of 'numerical representation'
as temperature on a thermometer.

3. Should any and every 'income difference' be reflected in a measure of inequality? The commonsense answer is
'No', for two basic reasons - need and merit. The first
reason is the more obvious: large families and the sick need
more resources than the single, healthy person to support
a particular economic standard. Hence in a 'just' allocation,
we would expect those with such greater needs to have a
higher income than other people; such income differences
would thus be based on a principle of justice, and should
not be treated as inequalities. To cope with this difficulty one may adjust the income concept such that
allowance is made for diversity of need, as mentioned in
the last section. The case for ignoring differences on
account of merit depends on the interpretation attached to
'equality'. One obviously rough and ready description of a
just allocation requires equal incomes for all irrespective
of personal differences other than need. However, one may
argue strongly that in a just allocation higher incomes
should be received by doctors, heroes, inventors,
Stakhanovites and other deserving persons. Unfortunately,
in practice it would be more difficult to make adjustments
similar to those suggested in the case of need and, more
generally, even distinguishing between income differences
that do represent genuine inequalities and those that do
not poses a serious problem.

4. The last point about the definition concerns the
phrase 'given population' and needs to be clarified in
two ways. Firstly, when examining the population over say
a number of years, what shall we do about the effect on

measured inequality of persons who either enter or leave the population, or whose status changes in some other relevant way? The usual assumption is that as long as the overall structure of income differences stays the same (regardless of whether different personnel are now receiving those incomes), measured inequality remains unaltered. Hence the phenomenon of social mobility within or in and out of the population eludes the conventional method of measuring inequality. Secondly, one is not exclusively concerned with inequality in the population as a whole. It is useful to be able to decompose this 'laterally' into inequality within constituent groups, differentiated regionally or demographically, perhaps, and inequality between these constituent groups. Indeed, once one acknowledges basic heterogeneities within the population, such as age or sex, awkward problems of aggregation may arise, although we shall ignore them. It may also be useful to decompose inequality 'vertically' so that one looks at inequality within a subgroup of the rich, or of the poor, for example. Hence the specification of the given population is by no means a trivial prerequisite to the application of inequality measurement.

Although the definition has made it clear that an inequality measure calls for a numerical scale, I have not suggested how this scale should be calibrated. Specific proposals for this will occupy the next two chapters, but a couple of obvious points can be made here. You may have noticed just now that the notion of justice was slipped in while income differences were being considered. That more just societies should register lower numbers on the inequality scale evidently accords with an intuitive appreciation of the term 'inequality'. Thus if we can clearly specify what a just distribution is, such a state provides the zero from which we start our inequality measure. However, even a well-defined principle of distributive justice is not sufficient to enable one to mark off an inequality scale unambiguously when considering diverse unequal social states. Each of the apparently contradictory scales I_1 and I_2 considered in the figure and the table might be solidly founded on the same principle of justice, unless such a principle were extremely narrowly defined.

The other general point is that we might suppose there is a close link between an indicator of the extent of poverty and the calibration of a measure of economic inequality. This is not necessarily so, because two rather different problems are generally involved. In the case of the measurement of poverty, one is concerned primarily with that section of the population falling below some specified 'poverty line'; to obtain the poverty measure one may perform a simple head count of this section, or calculate the gap between the average income of the poor and the average income of the general population, or carry out some other computation on poor people's incomes in relation to each other and to the rest of the population. Now in the case of inequality one generally wishes to capture the effects of income differences over a much wider range. Hence it is perfectly possible for the measured extent of poverty to be declining over time, while at the same time and in the same society measured inequality increases due to changes in income differences within the non-poor section of the population.

INEQUALITY AND THE SOCIAL STRUCTURE

Finally we return to the subject of the first ingredient, namely the basic social units used in studying
inequality – or the elementary particles of which we
imagine society to be constituted. The definition of the
social unit, whether it be a single person, the nuclear
family or the extended family depends intrinsically upon
the social context, and upon the interpretation of inequality that we impose. Although it may seem natural to
adopt an individualistic approach, some other 'collective
unit' may be more appropriate.

When *economic* inequality is our particular concern,
the theory of the development of the distribution of income
or wealth may itself influence the choice of the basic
social unit. To illustrate this, consider the classical
view of an economic system, the population being subdivided into distinct classes of workers, capitalists and
landowners. Each class is characterised by a particular
function in the economic order and by an associated type
of income – wages, profits, and rents. If, further, each
is regarded as internally fairly homogeneous, then it makes
sense to pursue the analysis of inequality in class terms
rather than in terms of individual units.

However, so simple a model is unsuited to describing
inequality in a significantly heterogeneous society, despite
the potential usefulness of class analysis for other social
problems. A superficial survey of the world around us
reveals rich and poor workers, failed and successful
capitalists and several people whose rôles and incomes do
not fit into neat slots. Hence the focus of attention in
this book is principally upon *individuals* rather than *types*
whether the analysis is interpreted in terms of economic

inequality or some other sense.

Thus reduced to its essentials it might appear that we are dealing with a purely formal problem, which sounds rather dull. This is not so. Although the subject matter of this book is largely technique, the techniques involved are essential for coping with the analysis of many social and economic problems in a systematic fashion; and these problems are far from dull or uninteresting.

2
Charting inequality I

F. Scott Fitzgerald: 'The rich are different from us.'
Ernest Hemingway: 'Yes, they have more money.'

If society really did consist of two or three fairly
homogeneous groups, economists could be saved a lot of
trouble. We could then simply look at the division of
income between landlords and peasants, among workers,
capitalists and rentiers, or any other appropriate
sections. Naturally we would still be faced with such
fundamental issues as how much each group *should* possess
or receive, whether the statistics are reliable and so on,
but questions such as 'what is the income distribution?'
could be satisfactorily met with a snappy answer '65% to
wages, 35% to profits'. Of course matters are not that
simple. As we have argued, we want a way of looking at
inequality that reflects both the depth of poverty of the
'have nots' of society and the height of well-being of
the 'haves': it is not easy to do this just by looking at
the income accruing to, or the wealth possessed by, two or
three groups. In the next three sections we will look at

several quite well-known ways of presenting inequality in a large heterogeneous group of people. To make the exposition easier I shall refer to 'income distribution', but you should bear in mind, of course, that the principles can be carried over to the distribution of any other variable that you can measure and that you think is of economic interest.

DIAGRAMS

There are several useful ways of representing inequality in picture form; the four that I shall discuss are introduced in italics below.

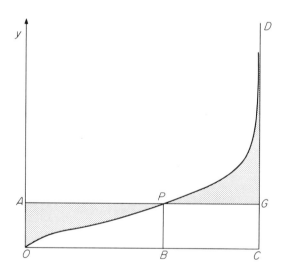

Source: Economic Trends, No. 272 (1976)
Distribution of incomes before tax,
U.K. 1973-74.

Figure 2-1

18

Pen's Parade. One of the most persuasive and attractive visual aids in the subject of income distribution has been developed by Jan Pen. Suppose that everyone in the population had a height proportional to his or her income. Line them up in order of height and let them march past in some given time interval - let us say one hour. Then the sight that meets our eyes is represented by the curve in figure 2-1. The whole parade passes in the interval represented by OC. But we do not meet the man with average income until we get to the point B (when well over half the parade has gone by). Average or mean income,[†] $\bar{y}$, is represented by the height OA. We have oversimplified Pen's original diagram by excluding from consideration people with negative reported incomes, which would involve the curve OD crossing the base line towards its left hand end. And in order to keep the diagram on the page, we have plotted the point D in a position that would be far too low in practice.

This diagram highlights the presence of any extremely large income and to a certain extent abnormally small incomes. But we may have reservations about the information it imparts concerning middle income receivers. We shall see this point recur when we use this diagram to derive an inequality measure that informs us about *changes* in the distribution.

Frequency distributions are well-tried tools of statisticians, and are discussed here mainly for the sake of completeness and as an introduction for those unfamiliar with the concept - for a fuller account see the references cited in the notes to this chapter. An example is found in

---

† This is simply total income divided by total population.

(a)

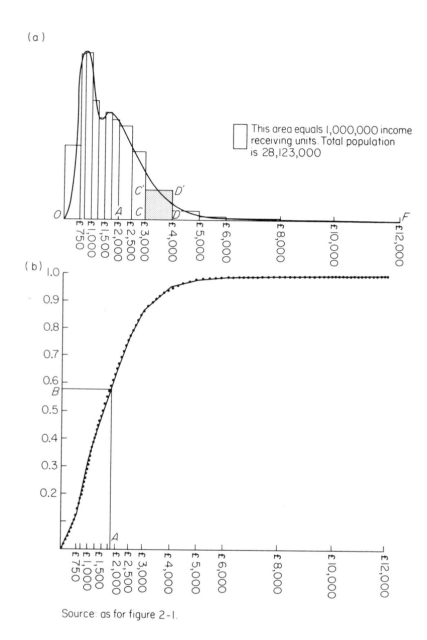

This area equals 1,000,000 income receiving units. Total population is 28,123,000

Source: as for figure 2-1.

Figure 2-2

figure 2-2a. Suppose you are looking down on a field. On one side, OF, there is a long straight fence marked off income categories: the physical distance between any two points such as C and D directly corresponds to the income differences they represent. Then get the whole population to come into the field and line up in the strip of land marked off by the piece of fence corresponding to their income bracket. So the £3,000-to-£4,000-a-year men stand on the patch $CDD'C'$. The shape that you get will resemble the stepped line in figure 2-2a – called a histogram – which represents the frequency distribution. It may be that we regard this as an empirical observation of a theoretical curve which describes the income distribution – for example the smooth curve drawn in figure 2-2a. The relationship $f(y)$ charted by this curve is sometimes known as a density function, where the scale is chosen such that the area under the curve and above the line OF is standardised at unity.

The frequency distribution shows what is happening in the middle income ranges more clearly. But perhaps it is not so readily apparent what is happening in the upper tail; indeed, in order to draw the figure, we have deliberately made the length OF much too short. (On the scale of this diagram it ought to be 100 metres at least!) This diagram and the 'Parade' are, however, intimately related; and we show this by constructing figure 2-2b from figure 2-2a. The horizontal scale of each figure is identical. On the vertical scale of figure 2-2b we plot 'cumulative frequency'. For any income y this cumulative frequency, written $F(y)$, is proportion to the *area* under the curve and to the left of y in figure 2-2a. If you experiment with the diagram you will see that as you increase y, $F(y)$ usually goes up (it can never decrease) — from a value of zero when you start at the lowest income received up to a value of one for the highest income. Thus, supposing we consider y = £3,000, we plot a point in figure 2-2b that corresponds to the proportion of the population with £3,000 *or less*. And we can repeat this operation for every point on either the empirical curve or on the smooth theoretical curve.

The visual relationship between figure 2-1 and figure 2-2b is now obvious. As a further point of reference, the position of mean income has been drawn in at the point A in the two figures. (If you still don't see it, try turning the page round!).

The Lorenz curve was introduced in 1905 as a powerful

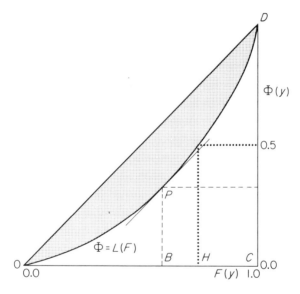

Source: as for figure 2-1

Figure 2-3

method of illustrating the inequality of the wealth distribution. An explanation may be given as follows.

Once again line up everybody in ascending order of incomes and let them parade by. Measure $F(y)$, the proportion of people who have passed by, along the horizontal axis of figure 2-3. Once point C is reached everyone has gone by, so $F(y) = 1.0$. Now as each person passes, hand him his share of the 'cake' - i.e. the proportion of total income that he receives. When the parade reaches people with income y, let us suppose that a proportion $\Phi(y)$ of the cake has gone. So of course when $F(y) = 0$, $\Phi(y)$ is also 0 (no cake gone); and when $F(y) = 1$, $\Phi(y)$ is also 1 (all the cake has been handed out). $\Phi(y)$ is measured on the vertical scale in figure 2-3, and the graph of Φ plotted against F is the Lorenz curve. Note that it is always convex toward the point C, the reason for which is easy to see. Suppose that the first 10% have filed by $(F(y_1) = .10)$ and you have handed out 4% of the cake $(\Phi(y_1) = .04)$; then by the time the next 10% of the people go by $(F(y_2) = .20)$, you *must* have handed out *at least* 8% of the cake $(\Phi(y_2) \geqslant .08)$. Why? - because we arranged the parade in ascending order of cake-receivers. Notice too that if the Lorenz curve lay along OD we would have a state of perfect equality, for along that line the first 5% get 5% of the cake, the first 10% get 10%.... and so on.

The relationship with figure 2-1 should again be evident. If we plot the slope of the Lorenz curve against the cumulative population proportions, F, then we are back precisely to Pen's Parade (scaled so that mean income equals unity). Once again, to facilitate comparison, the position where we meet the man with mean income has been marked as point B, although in the Lorenz diagram we cannot

23

represent mean income itself. Note that the mean occurs at a value of F such that the slope of the Lorenz curve is parallel to OD.

Logarithmic transformation. An irritating problem that arises in drawing the frequency curve of figure 2-2a is that we must either ignore some of the very large incomes in order to fit the diagram on the page, or put up with a diagram that obscures much of the detail in the middle and lower income ranges. We can avoid this to some extent by drawing a similar frequency distribution, but plotting the horizontal axis on a logarithmic scale as in figure 2-4.[†] Equal distances along OF correspond to equal *proportionate* income differences.

Again the point corresponding to mean income, $\bar{y}$, has been marked in as A. Note that the length OA equals $\log \bar{y}$ and is *not* the mean of the logarithms of income. This is marked in as the point A', so that the length $OA' = \log y*$ where $y*$ is the so-called geometric mean of the distribution. The geometric mean, found by taking the mean of the logarithms and then transforming back to natural numbers, can never exceed the (conventional) arithmetic mean.

We have now seen four different ways of presenting pictorially the same facts about income distribution. Evidently each graphical technique may emphasise quite different features of the distribution: the Parade draws attention to the enormous height of the well-off; the frequency curve presents middle incomes more clearly, the logarithmic transformation captures information from each

---

[†] Champernowne (1973, 1974) refers to this as the 'people curve'.

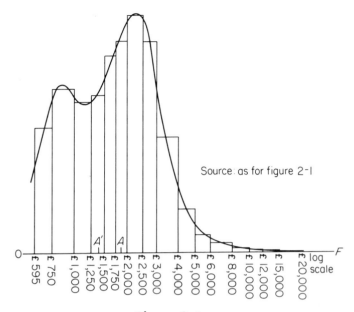

Figure values along axis: 595, 750, 1,000, 1,250, 1,500, 1,750, 2,000, 2,500, 3,000, 4,000, 5,000, 6,000, 8,000, 10,000, 12,000, 15,000, 20,000

log scale

A' A

Figure 2-4

of the 'tails' as well as the middle, but at the same
time sacrifices simplicity and ease of interpretation.
This difference in emphasis is partly reflected in the
inequality measures derived from the diagrams.

INEQUALITY MEASURES

We can use figures 2-1 to 2-4 to illustrate some
conventional inequality measures. The Parade itself
suggests two. Firstly, we have the *range*, which we define
simply as the distance *CD* in figure 2-1 or:

$$R = y_{max} - y_{min}$$

where y_{max} and y_{min} are, respectively the maximum and

25

minimum values of income in the parade (we may, of course standardise by considering R/y_{min} or $R/\bar{y}$. Plato had this concept in mind when he made the following judgement:

> We maintain that if a state is to avoid the greatest plague of all – I mean civil war, though civil disintegration would be a better term – extreme poverty and wealth must not be allowed to arise in any section of the citizen-body, because both lead to both these disasters. That is why the legislator must now announce the acceptable limits of wealth and poverty. The lower limit of poverty must be the value of the holding. The legislator will use the holding as his unit of measure and allow a man to possess twice, thrice, and up to four times its value.

The problems with the range are evident. Although it might be satisfactory in a small closed society where everyone's income is known fairly certainly, it is clearly unsuited to large, heterogeneous societies where the 'minimum' and 'maximum' incomes can at best only be guessed. The measure will be highly sensitive to the guesses or estimates of these two extreme values. Disregarding that, however, there is a more compelling reason for having doubts about the usefulness of R. Suppose we can wave a wand and bring about a society where the man at position O and the man at position C are left at the same height, but where everyone else in between was levelled to some equal, intermediate height. We would probably agree that inequality had been reduced, though not eliminated. But according to R it is just the same!

Unfortunately we snall find a similar criticism in subtler form attaches to the second inequality measure we can read off the Parade diagram – the so-called *relative mean deviation*. Look at the shaded portions in figure 2-1. These portions, which are necessarily of equal size,

constitute the area between the Parade-curve itself and
the horizontal line representing mean income. In some
sense, the larger is this area, the greater is
inequality. (Try drawing the Parade with more giants and
more dwarfs). It is conventional to standardise the
inequality measure in unit-free terms, so let us divide by
the total income (which equals area $OCGA$). Then the
relative mean deviation is defined as:

$$M = \frac{area\ OAP\ +\ area\ PGD}{area\ OCGA} \text{ }^{\dagger}$$

But now for the fatal weakness of M. Suppose you think that
the stature of the dwarfs to the left of B is socially
unacceptable. You arrange a reallocation of income so that
everyone with incomes below the mean (i.e. to the left of
point B) has exactly the same income. The parade then looks
like figure 2-5. But notice that the two shaded regions in

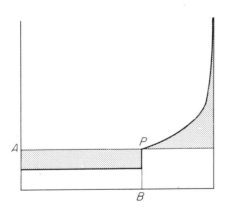

Figure 2-5

---

† You are invited to check the appendix for formal
  definitions of this and other equality measures.

figure 2-5 are *exactly* the same area as in figure 2-1: so
the value of M has not changed. Whatever reallocation you
arrange among people to the left of C only, or among
people to the right of C only, inequality according to the
relative mean deviation stays the same.

The relative mean deviation can be easily derived from
figure 2-3. From the formula in the appendix it can be
verified that $M = 2 [F(\bar{y}) - \Phi(\bar{y})]$, that is: $M = 2[OB - BP]$.
However a more common use of the diagram is to derive the
Gini concentration ratio, G, defined as the ratio of the
shaded area in figure 2-3 to the area OCD. The main
disadvantage of G is that an income transfer from a rich
man to a poor man has a much greater effect on G if the two
men are near the middle rather than at either end of the
parade. So, consider transferring £1 from a man with £1,100
to a man with £1,000. This has a much greater effect on
reducing G than transferring £1 from a man with £100 to one
with £0 or than transferring £1 from a man with £10,000 to
a man with £10,000. It is not evident that this is a
desirable property for an inequality measure to possess.

Other inequality measures can be derived from figure
2-3. Two have been suggested in connection with the problem
of measuring inequality in the distribution of power, as
reflected in voting strength. Firstly, consider the income
level y_O at which half the national cake has been
distributed to the parade; i.e. $\Phi(y_O) = \frac{1}{2}$. Then define the
minimal majority inequality measure as $F(y_O)$, i.e. as the
distance OH. If Φ is reinterpreted as the proportion of
seats in an elected assembly where the votes are spread
unevenly among the constituencies as reflected by the
Lorenz curve, and if F is reinterpreted as a proportion of
the electorate, then $1 - F(y_O)$ represents the smallest

proportion of the electorate that can secure a majority in the elected assembly. Secondly, we mention the *equal shares coefficient*. This is defined simply as $F(\bar{y})$; that is, the proportion of the population that has income $\bar{y}$ or less (the distance OB), or the proportion of the population that has 'average voting strength' or less. Clearly, either of these measures as applied to the distribution of income or wealth is subject to essentially the same criticism as the relative mean deviation. In the case of the first, it is insensitive to transfers among members of the Parade on the same side of the man with income y_O; in the case of the second it is insensitive to transfers among members of the Parade on the same side of the man with income $\bar{y}$.

Now let us consider figures 2-2 and 2-4. An obvious suggestion is to measure inequality in the same way as statisticians measure dispersion of any frequency distribution. In this application, the usual method would involve measuring the distance between the individual's income y_i and mean income $\bar{y}$, squaring this, and then finding the average of the resulting quantity in the whole population. Assuming that there are n people we define the *variance*:

$$V = \frac{1}{n} \sum_{i=1}^{n} [y_i - \bar{y}]^2$$

However, V is unsatisfactory in that were we simply to double everyone's incomes (and thereby double mean income and leave the shape of the distribution essentially unchanged), V would quadruple. One way round this problem is to standardize V. Define the *coefficient of variation* thus

$$c = \sqrt{V}/\bar{y}.$$

Another way to avoid the problem is to look at the variance in terms of the logarithms of income (i.e. from figure 2-4). There are two important definitions:

$$v = \frac{1}{n} \sum_{i=1}^{n} [\log(y_i/\bar{y})]^2$$

$$v_1 = \frac{1}{n} \sum_{i=1}^{n} [\log(y_i/y^*)]^2$$

The first we may call the *logarithmic variance*. The second we may term the *variance of the logarithms of incomes*. Note that v is defined relative to the *logarithm of mean income*; v_1 is defined relative to the *mean of the logarithm of income*. Either definition is invariant under proportional increases in all incomes.[†]

We shall find that v_1 has much to recommend it when we come to examine the lognormal distribution in Chapter 4. However c, v and v_1 can be criticised more generally on grounds similar to those on with G was criticised. Consider a transfer of £1 from a man with y to a man with y - £100 . How does this affect these inequality measures? In the case of c, it does not matter in the slightest where in the parade this transfer is effected: so whether the transfer is from a man with £500 to a man with £400, or from a man with £10,100 to a man with £10,000, the reduction in c is exactly the same. Thus c will be particularly good at capturing inequality among high incomes, but may be of more limited use in reflecting inequality elsewhere in the distribution.

---

† Those who are mathematically inclined may care to note that
$$v = v_1 + [\log(y^*/\bar{y})]^2$$

In contrast to this property of c, there appears to be good reason to suggest that a measure of inequality have the property that a transfer of the above type carried out in the low income brackets would be quantitatively more effective in reducing inequality than if the transfer were carried out in the high income brackets. The measures v and v_1 appear to go some way toward meeting this objection. Taking the example of figures 2-1 to 2-4 (where we have $\bar{y}$ = £1,857), a transfer of £1 from a man with £1,100 to a man with £1,000 reduces v or v_1 less than a transfer of £1 from a man with £500 to a man with £400. But, unfortunately, v and v_1 'overdo' this effect, so to speak. For if we consider a transfer from a man with £10,100 to a man with £10,000 inequality, as measured by v or v_1, *increases*! This is hardly a desirable property for an inequality measure to possess, even if it does occur only at high incomes.[†]

Other statistical properties of the frequency distribution may be pressed into service as inequality indices. While these may draw attention to particular aspects of inequality - such as dispersion among the very high or very low incomes, by and large they miss the point as far as *general* inequality of incomes is concerned. Consider, for example, measures of skewness. For symmetrical distributions (such as the Normal curve) these measures are zero; but this zero value of the measure may be consistent with either a very high or a very low dispersion of incomes (as measured by the coefficient of variation). This does not appear to capture the essential ideas of inequality measurement.

---

† You will *always* get this trouble if the 'poorer' of the two men has at least 2.72 times mean income $\bar{y}$ - see the appendix.

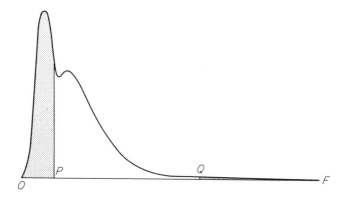

Figure 2-6

Figure 2-2 can be used to derive an inequality measure
from quite a different source Stark (1972) has argued that
an appropriate practical method of measuring inequality
should be based on society's revealed judgements on the
definition of poverty and riches. The method is best seen
by redrawing figure 2-2 as figure 2-6. Since Stark's study
concentrated specifically on UK incomes we shall also
discuss the issue in terms of this application. The distance
OP in figure 2-6 we will call the range of 'low incomes'. In
the case of the UK, P is fixed from the basic national
assistance (supplementary benefit) scale plus a percentage
to allow for underestimation of income and income
disregarded in applying for assistance. The distance QF we
will call the range of 'high incomes'. The point Q is
determined by the level at which one becomes liable to
surtax, adjusted for need.[†] Stark's *high/low* index is then

---

[†] Note that in a practical application, the positions of
both P and Q depend on family composition. This however,
is a point which we are deferring until later. Figure 2-6
illustrates one typical case.

computed by dividing the sum of the two shaded areas by the total area between the curve and the line OF.

Stark's measure is at once imaginative and practical, but it suffers from three important weaknesses. Firstly, it is subject to exactly the same type of criticism that we levelled against M, and against the 'minimal majority' and 'equal share' measures. The measure is completely insensitive to transfers *among* the 'poor', *among* the 'rich' or *among* the 'middle income receivers'. Secondly, there is an awkward dilemma concerning the behaviour of points P and Q over time. Suppose one leaves them fixed in relative terms - i.e. that OP increases only at the same rate as mean income increases over time. Then one faces the criticism that one's current criterion for measuring inequality is based on an arbitrary standard fixed, perhaps, a quarter of a century ago. On the other hand, suppose that OP increases with year-to-year increases in the social standard of reference - i.e. the national assistance scales (with a similar argument affecting the movement of point Q). Then if the inequality measure shows a rising trend because of more people falling in the 'low income' category, one must face the criticism that this is just an optical illusion created by altering the definitions of 'poor' people. Some compromise between the two courses must be chosen and the results derived for a particular application treated with caution. Thirdly, there is the point that in practice the contribution of the shaded area in the upper tail to the inequality measure is negligible. Then the behaviour of the inequality measure is dominated by what happens in the lower tail - which may or may not be an acceptable feature - and simplifies effectively to whether people 'fall in' on the right or on

the left of point P when we arrange them in the frequency
distribution diagram (figures 2-2a and 2-6).

The use of any one of the measures we have discussed in
this section implies certain value judgements concerning
the way we compare one person's income against that of
another. The detail of such judgements will be explained in
the next chapter, although we have already seen a glimpse
of some of the issues.

'NON-DECISIVE' APPROACHES

Finally we consider ways of looking at inequality that
may lead to ambiguous results. Let us say straight away that
this is not necessarily a bad thing. It may be helpful to
know that over a particular period events have altered the
income distribution so that one finds offsetting effects on
the amount of inequality. The measures which we have
examined in the previous section act as 'tie-breakers' in
such an event. Each resolves the ambiguity in its own
particular way. Just how we *should* resolve these ambiguities
is taken up more closely in the next chapter. We will now
look at two related non-decisive approaches.

The first method is the Lorenz curve itself. An
interesting question to ask in comparing two distributions
is - does the Lorenz curve of the one lie wholly 'inside'
(i.e. closer to the line of perfect equality than) the
other? If it does, then we should have no difficulty in
securing agreement that the 'inside' curve represents a
more evenly-spread distribution. To see this point, examine
figure 2-7. Suppose that in year A income distribution is
represented by the Lorenz curve marked A. A few years later
(year B) we find the distribution changed such that B is now
the appropriate curve. Observe that if we consider any

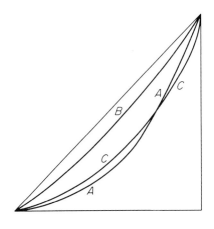

Figure 2-7

'bottom proportion' of people $F(y)$, they get a larger share
of the cake $\Phi(y)$ in B than in A. So whereas the bottom 30%
get 7% of the cake in A, they get 22% in B; the bottom 50%
get 18% of the cake in A, but 40% in B; the bottom 95% get
91% of the cake in A, but 94% in B. So if we are in favour
of greater equality we shall readily agree that B is a
better situation than A; and as it happens, all our
foregoing inequality measures (except, just possibly, v and
v_1) will indicate that inequality has gone down.

Unfortunately, it is only on rare occasions that we can
obtain this happy result. If the Lorenz curves intersect,
then we cannot say whether inequality has increased or
decreased – we have to use a tie-breaker. This situation is
illustrated by curves A and C. In year C, the bottom 5% get
a larger proportion of the cake than they do in year A; the
bottom 10% are also relatively better off. But the bottom
80% get a *smaller* proportion of the cake in year C than
they do in year A (i.e. the top 20% are better off) – in

35

going from A to C there has been a redistribution away from middle income receivers to the top *and* to the bottom. Whether this is a 'good thing' depends on how we weight the two simultaneous transfers, and different single-valued inequality measures will give different answers.

Now let us turn to the second device, commonly referred to as 'the method of percentiles', and also formalised in terms of a 'comparative function'. The technique only requires a simple redrawing of figure 2-1 or figure 2-2b as an expository device, as in figure 2-8a. On the vertical axis we measure percentages of the population, and horizontally we have income – for convenience's sake plotted on a log scale. Consider curve A: for any level of income we select, the ordinate P shows us the percentage of the population with *that income or more,* so that $P = 1 - F(y)$. Conversely we can look at a given 'percentile' – for example the top 40% – and from curve A read off on the abscissa the *minimum* income the top 40% must possess (in the case of curve A, this is £1,000). Suppose we consider another curve B, drawn in the same way for a second distribution. The 'comparative function' is defined as the distance $K(P)$ for any 100.P percentile. So choose a percentile (let us say the 40th), determine the minimum income of the top 40% in year A (say £y_A) and the minimum income of the top 40% in year B (say £y_B), then $K(40\%) = \log(y_A/y_B)$.

Let us see how this assists us in charting the change in inequality. Examine figure 2-8b. Instead of comparing just two distributions we are now looking at indefinitely many over a period 1938 to 1957. So the distributions have not been drawn in, only the values of the comparative functions for particular percentiles are plotted against time. Each curve represents $K_t(P)$, the comparative function

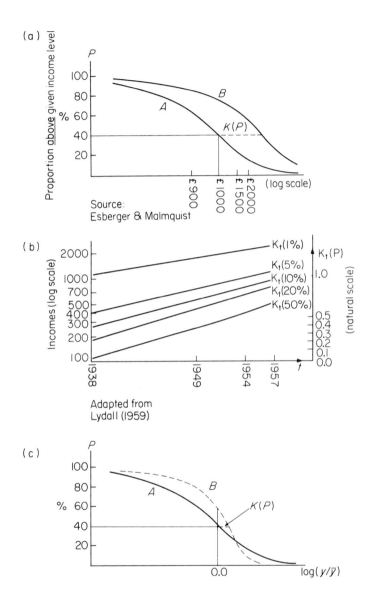

(a)

Proportion **above** given income level

P

100
80   *B*
% 60
40   *K(P)*
20

                £900 £1000 £1500 £2000   (log scale)

Source:
Esberger & Malmquist

(b)

Incomes (log scale)

2000   Kₜ(1%)   Kₜ(P)
                                        Kₜ(5%)
1000   Kₜ(10%)   1.0
700   Kₜ(20%)
500
400   Kₜ(50%)
300
200   0.5
                                                  0.4
                                                  0.3
100   0.2
                                                  0.1
                                                  0.0

1938   1949   1954   1957 *t*

(natural scale)

Adapted from
Lydall (1959)

(c)

P

100
80   *B*
% 60   *A*
40   *K(P)*
20

            0.0   log(*y*/ȳ)

Figure 2-8

37

for a particular P, computed from the income distribution at date t and compared with an arbitary equal distribution of £100 in 1938. Thus on the *left-hand* scale we can read off the income of a representative man at the bottom of the Pth percentile in a particular year. So the man at the 20th percentile received £185 in 1938: in 1949 he received £430. On the *right-hand* scale we read off the corresponding K - values. $K(20\%) \approx 0.27$ in 1938; $K(20\%) \approx 0.63$ in 1949. Using the Ks, we can easily read off the growth rate of any percentile. For example, $K_{1949}(20\%) - K_{1938}(20\%) \approx .36$. Checking a K - value of .36 against the left-hand scale we read the value £230 (approximately). This tells us that for the hypothetical man at the 20th percentile, every £100 of income he had in 1938 would have grown to about £230 in 1949; i.e. his income had grown by 130%. From this exercise, we see that the choice of base and of base year for measuring the Ks is not restrictive, since we can easily compute the comparative function using the actual distribution of 1949 as a base, we simply read off $K_{1949}^{1957}(5\%) = K_{1957}(5\%) - K_{1949}(5\%)$. Now is the distribution in 1957 more 'equal' than the distribution in 1949? It would seem reasonable to answer affirmatively if $K_{1949}^{1957}(P)$ always gets larger as we consider larger P. This means that the proportional gain of a representative person at the bottom of the 'top 50%' bracket is larger than the proportional gain of a representative person at the bottom of the 'top 40%' bracket, which is in turn larger than the gain at the bottom of the 'top 30%' bracket - and so on. So if *all* the curves in figure 2-8b seem to 'converge' toward the right-hand end, we conclude that incomes are becoming more equal. But of course, if $K_{1949}^{1957}(1\%) < K_{1949}^{1957}(50\%)$ *but*

$K_{1949}^{1957}(50\%) > K_{1949}^{1957}(90\%)$ we cannot say immediately whether inequality is decreasing or not. Not all the curves are converging, and though the middle income brackets have 'caught up' on the top brackets, they have also 'pulled away from' the lower brackets.

It is interesting to examine the relationship between the method of percentiles (the comparative function) and the Lorenz curve method. In order to do this we need to *standardise* the comparative function, since the value of $K(P)$ is obviously sensitive to changes in the mean of the whole distribution. Thus we have to relabel the horizontal axis of figure 2-8a as $\log(y/\bar{y})$ where $\bar{y}$ is the mean of the distribution – see figure 2-8c. We will now find that the two distributions *must* intersect (whether or not distribution A is unambiguously more/less equal than curve B). Then it is easy to establish the following (for the original non-standardised function $K(P)$ of figure 2-8a).

1. If $K(P)$ is everywhere increasing in P, then the Lorenz curve of distribution A lies wholly 'inside' the Lorenz curve of B.

2. If for some P the rate of increase of K with respect to P becomes zero ($dK(P)/dP = 0$), then at that value of P we will find that the Lorenz curves intersect.

We have seen how a large number of *ad hoc* inequality measures are associated with various diagrams that chart inequality which are themselves all interlinked. But however appealing each pictorial representation might be, we find that we would have important reservations about any of the associated inequality measures. The techniques of this section, although indecisive in themselves, provide a useful introduction to the deeper analysis of inequality measurement to be found in the next chapter.

3
Charting inequality II

'He's half a millionaire: he has the
air but not the million.'

- Jewish Proverb

In the last chapter we looked at measures of inequality
that came about more or less by accident. In some cases a
concept was borrowed from statistics and pressed into
service as a tool of inequality measurement. In others a
useful diagrammatic device was used to generate a measure
of inequality that 'naturally' seemed to fit it (for
example, the relative mean deviation and the Parade; or
the Gini coefficient and the Lorenz curve).

However, if we were to follow the dull, analytical
course of rejecting visual intuition, and of constructing
an inequality measure from 'first principles', what approach
should we adopt? I shall outline two possibilities, and in
doing so consider mainly special cases that illustrate the
main points easily without pretending to be analytically
rigorous. The first method we shall examine is that of
deriving inequality measures from social welfare functions.
The social welfare function itself may be supposed to

subsume values of society regarding equality and justice, and thus the derived inequality measures are given a normative basis. The second approach is to specify a set of axioms sufficient to determine an inequality measure uniquely; the choice of axioms themselves, of course, will be determined by what we think an inequality measure 'should' look like. This is shown to be related to concepts in information theory.

SOCIAL WELFARE FUNCTIONS

An obvious way of introducing social values concerning inequality is to use a social welfare function (SWF) which simply ranks all the possible states of society in the order of (society's) preference. The various 'states' could be functions of all sorts of things – personal income, wealth, size of people's cars – but we usually attempt to isolate certain characteristics which are considered 'relevant' in situations of social choice. We do not have to concern ourselves here with the means by which this social ranking is derived. The ranking may be handed down by parliament, imposed by a dictator, suggested by the trade unions, or simply thought up by the observing economist – the key point is that its characteristics are carefully specified in advance, and that these characteristics can be criticised on their own merits.

In its simplest form, a SWF simply orders social states unambiguously: if state A is preferable to state B then (and only then) the SWF has a higher value for state A than that for state B. How may we construct a useful SWF? Let us list some qualities that it may be desirable for a SWF to possess; their significance is discussed later. First introduce a preliminary piece of notation: y_{iA} is the magnitude of person i's 'economic position' in social state A, where i is a label that can be any number between 1 and n inclusive. For example, y_{iA} could be the income of Mr Jones of Potter's Bar in the year 1968. (Where it does not matter, the A-suffix will be dropped). Then define the following five characteristics of the SWF.

1. The SWF is *individualistic* and *nondecreasing*, if for any state A: $W_A = W(y_{1A}, y_{2A}, \ldots, y_{nA})$ and if $y_{iB} \geqslant y_{iA}$ implies, *ceteris paribus*, that $W_B \geqslant W_A$, which in turn implies that state B is at least as good as state A.

2. The SWF is *symmetric* for any state if it is true that $W(y_1, y_2, \ldots, y_n) = W(y_2, y_1, \ldots, y_n) = \ldots = W(y_n, \ldots, y_2, y_1)$. That is, the value of W does not depend on the particular assignment of labels to members of the population.

3. The SWF is *additive* if it can be written $W(y_1, y_2, \ldots, y_n) = \sum_{i=1}^{n} U_i(y_i) = U_1(y_1) + U_2(y_2) + \ldots + U_n(y_n)$, where U_1 is a function of y_1 alone, etc.

If properties 1 to 3 are all satisfied then we can write $W = U(y_1) + U(y_2) + \ldots + U(y_n)$, where U is the same function for each man and where $U(y_i)$ increases with y_i. If attention is restricted to this *special* case the last two definitions can be simplified, since they may be expressed in terms of U alone. Let us call $U(y_1)$ the social utility of, or the *welfare index* for, man 1. The rate at which this index increases is $U'(y_1) = dU(y_1)/dy_1$, social marginal utility of, or the *welfare weight* for man 1. Notice that because of property 1, none of the welfare weights can be negative.

4. The SWF is strictly *concave* if the welfare weight always decreases as y_i increases.

5. The SWF has *constant elasticity*, or *constant relative inequality aversion* if $U(y_i)$ can be written $U(y_i) = \frac{1}{1-\varepsilon} y_i^{1-\varepsilon}$ (or in a cardinally equivalent form), where ε is the *inequality aversion parameter* (which is non-negative).

It must be emphasised that this is a *very* abbreviated discussion of the properties of SWFs, and for a thorough treatment the reader should consult the references in the notes to this chapter. However these five basic points are sufficient to derive a convenient purpose-built inequality measure, and thus we shall examine their significance more closely.

The first point simply states that the welfare numbers should be related to individual incomes (or wealth, etc.) so that if any man's income goes up social welfare cannot go down. The term 'individualistic' may be applied to the case where the SWF is defined in relation to the *satisfactions* people derive from their income, rather than the incomes themselves. I shall ignore this point and assume that any standardisation of the incomes, y_i, (for example to allow for differing needs) has already been performed.[†] This permits a straightforward comparison of the individual levels, and of differences in individual levels, of people's 'economic position' - represented by the y_i and loosely called 'income'. Given that we treat these standardised incomes y_i as a measure that puts everyone in the population on an equal footing as regards needs and deserts,

---

† Attention is once again drawn to my loose use of the word 'person'. In practice incomes may be received by households of differing sizes, in which case the y_i must be reinterpreted as *per capita* equivalent incomes. This is taken up in Chapter 5.

condition 2 naturally follows - there is no reason why
welfare should be higher or lower if any two people simply
'swapped incomes'.

The third assumption is quite strong, and is independent
of the second. Suppose you measure $W_B - W_A$, the increase in
welfare from state A to state B, where the only change is
an increase in man 1's income from £2,000 to £3,000. Then
assumption 3 states that the effect of this change alone
(increasing man 1's income from £2,000 to £3,000) is quite
independent of what the rest of state A looked like - it
does not matter whether everyone else had £1 or £10,000,
$W_B - W_A$ is just the same for this particular change. However
this convenient assumption is not as restrictive in terms
of resulting inequality measures as it might seem at first
sight - this will become clearer when the concept of
'distance' between income shares is considered later in
this chapter.

It is possible to phrase assumption 4 in much more
general terms, but discussion is easier in terms of the
welfare index U. Note that this is *not* an ordinary
utility function, although it may have very similar
properties - it represents the valuation given by *society*
of a man's income. One may think of this as a 'social
utility function'. In this case, the concept corresponding
to 'social marginal utility', is the quantity $U'(y_i)$ which
we have called the *welfare weight*. The reason for the
latter term is as follows. Consider a government programme
which brings about a (small) change in everyone's income:
$\Delta y_1, \Delta y_2, \ldots, \Delta y_n$. What is the change in social welfare?
It is simply $\Delta W = U'(y_1) . \Delta y_1 + U'(y_2) . \Delta y_2 + \ldots + U'(y_n) .$
Δy_n, so the U'-quantities act as a system of weights
when summing the effects of the programme over the whole

population. How should the weights be fixed? Assumption 4 (strict concavity) tells us that the higher a man's income, the lower the social weight he is given. If we are averse to inequality this seems reasonable – a small redistribution from rich to poor should lead to a socially-preferred state.

It is possible to obtain powerful results simply with assumptions 1 to 4. By restricting the U-function, however, assumption 5 turns the SWF into a very useful tool. If a man's income increases, we know (from assumption 4) that his welfare weight (necessarily) decreases – but by how much? Assumption 5 states that the proportional decrease in the weight U' for a given proportional increase in income should be the same at any income level. So if a man's income increases 1% (from £100 to £101, or £10,000 to £10,100) his welfare weight drops by ε% of its former value. The higher ε, the faster the rate of proportional decline in welfare weight to proportional increase in income – hence its name as the 'inequality aversion parameter'. The number ε describes the strength of our yearning for equality *vis à vis* uniformly higher income for all. A simple numerical illustration may help. Consider a rich man R with five times the income of poor man P. Our being inequality averse certainly implies that we approve of a redistribution of exactly £1 from R to P – i.e. with no net loss of income. But we may approve of the transfer even if it is going to cost R more than £1 in order to give £1 to P – in fact we are prepared (in this case) to allow a sacrifice of up to £5$^{\varepsilon}$ by R to make a transfer of £1 to P. So,

if $\varepsilon = 0$ we agree to take £1.00 off R to give £1 to P;
if $\varepsilon = \frac{1}{2}$ "   "   "   " £2.24 " R "   " £1 to P;

if ε = 1 we agree to take £5.00 off R to give £1 to P;
if ε = 2 "   "   "   " £25.00 " R " " £1 to P;

... and so on. If we consider an indefinitely large value of
ε, we give *total* priority to equality over any objective
of raising incomes generally. Social welfare is determined
simply by the position of the least advantaged in society.

Five social welfare functions satisfying conditions 1
to 5 are illustrated in figure 3-1a. The case ε = 0 illustrates that of a concave, but not strictly concave SWF; all

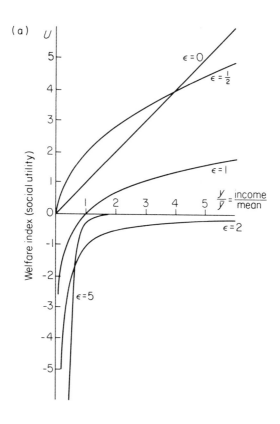

Figure 3-1a

the other curves in the figure represent strictly concave
SWFs. The figure illustrates the point that for values of
ε less than unity, the SWF is 'bounded below' but not
'bounded above': from the ε = $\frac{1}{2}$ curve we see that with
this SWF no one is ever assigned a welfare index lower than
zero, but there is no upper limit on the welfare index
that can be assigned to an individual. Conversely, for ε
greater than unity, the SWF is bounded above, but unbounded
below: if someone's income approaches zero, then we can
assign him an indefinitely large *negative* social utility
(welfare index), but no matter how large a man's income
is, he will never be assigned a welfare index greater than
zero. Notice that the vertical scale of this diagram is
fairly arbitrary. We could multiply the *U*-values by any
positive number, and add (or subtract) any constant to the
U-values without altering their characteristics as welfare
indices. The essential characteristic of the different
welfare scales represented by these curves is the *elasticity* of the function $U(y)$ or, loosely speaking, the
curvature of the different graphs, related to the parameter ε. For convenience, I have chosen the units of income
so that the mean is now unity: in other words, original
income is expressed as a proportion of the mean. If these
units are changed, then we have to change the vertical
scale for *each* *U*-curve individually, but when we come to
computing inequality measures using this type of *U*-function,
the choice of units for *y* is immaterial.

The system of welfare weights (social marginal utilities) implied by these *U*-funtions is illustrated in figure
3-1b, which for convenience has been drawn with a logarithmic vertical scale. Notice that for every ε > 0, the
welfare weights fall as income increases. Notice in

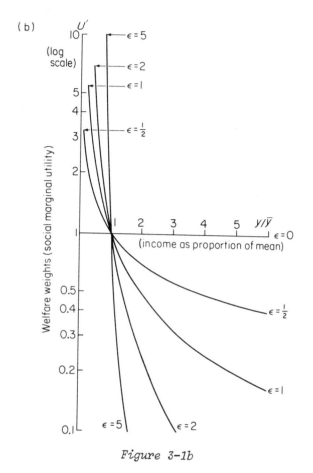

Figure 3-1b

particular how rapid this fall is once one reached an ε-value of only 5: evidently one's income has only to be about 63% of the mean in order to be assigned a welfare weight 10 times as great as the weight of the man at mean income.

Let us now put the concept of the SWF to work. A very important result, which does *not* require assumption 5, can be established for additively separable, concave SWFs.

THEOREM 1 Let the social state A have an associated income distribution $(y_{1A}, y_{2A}, \ldots, y_{nA})$ and social state B have income distribution $(y_{1B}, y_{2B}, \ldots, y_{nB})$, where total income in state A and in state B is identical. Let W be *any* SWF satisfying assumptions 1 to 4. Then the Lorenz curve for state B lies wholly inside the Lorenz curve for state A *if and only if* $W_B > W_A$ for every SWF satisfying assumptions 1 to 4.

This shows at once the power of the Lorenz diagram, and the relevance of SWFs of the type we have discussed. Re-examine figure 2-7. We found that intuition suggested that curve B represented a 'fairer' or 'more equal' distribution than curve A. This may be made more precise. Assumptions 1 to 4 crystallise our views that social welfare should depend on individual economic position, and that we should be averse to inequality. Theorem 1 reveals the identity of this approach with the intuitive method of the Lorenz diagram, subject to the 'constant amount of cake' assumption introduced in Chapter 1. Notice that this does not depend on the assumption that our relative aversion to inequality should be the same for all income ranges - other concave forms of the U-function would do. Also it is possible to weaken assumptions 1 to 4 considerably (but at the expense of ease of exposition) and leave theorem 1 intact. Moreover the result of theorem 1 can be extended to some cases where the cake does not stay the same size - the notes to this chapter discuss these points further.

However, this theorem is not sufficient for the practical business of inequality measurement. In the first place, Lorenz curves that we wish to compare often intersect. In the second place we desire a unique numerical value for inequality in order to make comparisons of different *changes* in inequality referred to in Chapter 1. So we use the SWF to find measures of inequality.

SWF-BASED INEQUALITY MEASURES

From figure 3-1 we can derive two important classes of inequality measure. To see how this is done, examine figure 3-2, which is really three diagrams superimposed

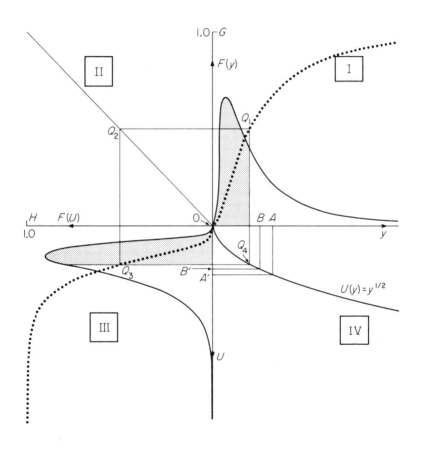

Figure 3-2

for convenience. In quadrant IV we have plotted one of
the 'welfare-index', or 'social utility' curves from
figure 3-1, which of course requires the use of assumption
5.[†] In quadrant I you will recognise the density function
or frequency distribution for the data under consideration
and, superimposed on it, the cumulative frequency distribution. These are drawn for income or wealth in the usual
way (cf figures 2-2a and 2-2b). We want to construct similar
curves for *the distribution of social utility or welfare
index, U*. To do this we use the cumulative distribution
function and the curve of quadrant IV. Pick any y-value
(income); read off the corresponding F-value (proportion
of population) on OG and the corresponding U-value (social
utility) on OU. Now plot the F and U-values in a new
diagram (quadrant III) - this is done by using quadrant II
just to reflect OG on to OH. What we have done is to map
the point Q_1 in quadrant I into the point Q_3 in quadrant
III. If we do this for other y-values and points on the
quadrant I cumulative frequency distribution, we end up
with a new cumulative frequency distribution in quadrant
III. (To see how this works, try tracing round another set
of points like $Q_1 \ Q_2 \ Q_3 \ Q_4$.) Once we have this new cumulative frequency distribution in terms of social utility,
we easily derive the frequency distribution itself in terms
of social utility - which is the solid curve in quadrant
III. Notice the equality of the two shaded areas for a
particular pair of y- and U-values.

---

† In order to keep the diagram manageable, we have chosen a
U-curve with $\varepsilon < 1$, so that it is bounded below and thus
fits neatly in one quadrant. The derivation of inequality
measures works for any $\varepsilon \geqslant 0$, but for $\varepsilon \geqslant 1$ the diagram
becomes untidy and Dalton's measure needs to be reinter-
preted - see the discussion below.

Now let us derive the inequality measures. For the distribution of income mark the position of the mean, $\bar{y}$, in the same fashion as Chapter 2, as point A on Oy. Do the same for the distribution of social utility - point B' on OU. We can also mark in two other points of interest (i) the social utility corresponding to $\bar{y}$ - we do this using the curve in quadrant IV and plotting point A' on OU; (ii) the income corresponding to average social utility - we do this by a reverse process using quadrant IV and plotting point B on Oy. The distance OA' represents the social utility for each person in the community were national income to be distributed perfectly equally. The distance OB represents the income which, if received by each member of the community, would result in the same level of social welfare as the existing distribution yields. Call this y_e. Necessarily $y_e \lesssim \bar{y}$ - we may be able to throw some of the national income away, redistribute the rest equally and still end up with the same level of social welfare. Notice that we have drawn the diagram for a particular isoelastic utility function in quadrant IV; if ε were changed, then so would the frequency distribution of quadrant III, and of course the positions of B and B'.

Thus we can define a different inequality measure for each value of ε, the inequality aversion parameter. An intuitively appealing way of measuring inequality seems to be to consider how far *actual* average social utility falls short of *potential* average social utility (if all income were distributed equally). So we define *Dalton's Inequality Index* (for inequality aversion ε) as:

$$D_\varepsilon = 1 - \frac{OB'}{OA'}$$

We note that this is zero for perfectly equally distributed

incomes ($OB' = OA'$) and unity if one man receives all the income ($OB' = 0$), as long as $\varepsilon < 1$. Atkinson (1970) criticises the use of D_ε on the grounds that it is sensitive to the level from which social utility is measured – if you add a non-zero constant to all the Us, D_ε changes.[†] Now this does not change the *ordering* properties of D_ε over different distributions, but the inequality measures obtained by adding different arbitrary constants to U will not be cardinally equivalent. So Atkinson suggests, in effect, that we perform our comparisons back on the Oy axis, not the OU axis, and compare the 'equally distributed equivalent' income, y_e, with the mean. So define *Atkinson's Inequality Index* (for inequality aversion ε) as

$$A_\varepsilon = 1 - \frac{OB}{OA} \; .$$

Once again this varies between zero and one, and also like D_ε, we find a different value of A_ε for different values of our aversion to inequality.

It is possible to check from the definitions in the appendix that the following relationship holds for all distributions and all values of ε (other than unity):

$$1 - D_\varepsilon = [1 - A_\varepsilon]^{1-\varepsilon}$$

Clearly as long as ε is less than one,[¶] the choice between D_ε and A_ε as defined above is only of vital importance with respect to their cardinal properties ('is the reduction in inequality by taxation greater in year A than in year B?'); they are obviously ordinally equivalent in that they

---

† As long as $\varepsilon \neq 1$, D_ε is not sensitive to the *units* in which it is measured as you can check by multiplying all the U-values by some positive constant i.e. just 'stretch' the line OU in figure 3-2.

¶ Footnote over page

produce the same *ranking* of different distributions. Of
much greater significance is the choice of the value of ε,
especially where Lorenz curves intersect, as do curves A
and C in figure 2-7. This reflects our relative sensitivity
to redistribution from the rich to the not-so-rich *vis à vis*
redistribution from the not-so-poor to the poor. If a low
value of ε is used we are particularly sensitive to changes
in distribution at the top end of the parade; if a high
value is employed, then it is the bottom end of the parade
which concerns us most - a numerical example of this is
found at the end of this chapter. The advantage of the
SWF approach is evident. Once agreed on the *form* of the
SWF (e.g. along the lines of assumptions one to five) it
enables the analyst of inequality to say, in effect 'you
tell me how strong society's aversion to inequality is,
and I will tell you the value of the inequality statistic',
rather than simply incorporating an arbitrary social
weighting in an inequality index that just happens to be
convenient.

Footnote from previous page
¶ Dalton's measure requires reinterpretation for $\varepsilon \gtrless 1$. If
we define D_1 as $1 - \log(y^*)/\log(\bar{y})$ where y^* is the geometric mean, we see that D_1 can easily exceed unity, and
indeed is unbounded above. Likewise, if we consider the
case $\varepsilon > 1$ we find that instead of lying between zero and
unity D_ε lies between 0 and $-\infty$. In order to transform this
into an inequality measure that is comparable with others
we have used, it would be necessary to look at values of
$D_\varepsilon/[D_\varepsilon - 1]$. One might be tempted to suggest that as long
as inequality aversion is less than unity, D_ε is as
suitable a choice as A_ε. However, even if ε lies between
zero and one, certain unsatisfactory features of D_ε
appear. For Atkinson's measure, A_ε, the higher is the
value of ε, the greater is the value of the inequality
measure for any given distribution. But this does not
hold for D_ε, even for ε in the zero-to-one range, an
assertion which is proved in the appendix.

INEQUALITY AND INFORMATION THEORY

Probability distributions sometimes provide useful analogies for income distributions. In this section we shall see that usable and quite reasonable inequality measures may be built up from an analogy with information theory.

In information theory, one is concerned with the problem of 'valuing' the information that a certain event out of a large number of possibilities has occurred. Let us suppose that there are events numbered 1, 2, 3 ..., to which we attach probabilities p_1, p_2, p_3, ... Each p is not less that zero (which represents total impossibility of the event's occurrence) and not greater than one (which represents absolute certainty of the event's occurrence). Suppose we are told that event no 1 has occurred – we want to assign a number $h(p_1)$ to this information – how do we do this? If event no 1 was quite likely anyway (p_1 near to 1), the information is not fiercely exciting, and so we want $h(p_1)$ rather low; if event 1 was a near impossibility, then this information is amazing and valuable – it gets a high $h(p_1)$. So $h(p_1)$ decreases as p_1 increases. A further characteristic which it seems correct that $h(.)$ should have (in the context of *probability* analysis) is as follows. If event 1 and event 2 are statistically independent (i.e. the probability that event 1 occurs does not depend on whether or not event 2 occurs, and *vice versa*), then the probability that *both* event 1 *and* event 2 occur together is $p_1 p_2$. So, if we want to be able to add up the information values of messages concerning independent events, we want h to have the property $h(p_1 p_2) = h(p_1) + h(p_2)$, and the function that satisfies this is $h = - \log p$.

However, a set of n numbers – the probabilities relating to each of n possible states – is in itself an unwieldy thing with which to work. It is convenient to aggregate these into a single number which describes whether the entire system is more or less 'orderly'. This is done by calculating the average information content of the system – i.e. the weighted sum of all the information values for the various events.

The weights used are the probabilities of the events themselves, and the resulting average is known as the *entropy* of the system. So

$$\text{entropy equals} \sum_{i=1}^{n} p_i \; h(p_i) = - \sum_{i=1}^{n} p_i \; \log(p_i)$$

Now Theil has argued that the entropy concept provides a useful device for inequality measurement. All we have to do is reinterpret the n possible events as n people in the population, and reinterpret p_i as the share of man i in total income, let us say s_i, where of course if $\bar{y}$ is mean income, and y_i is the income of man i, $s_i = y_i/n\bar{y}$, so that $\Sigma s_i = 1$. Then subtracting the actual entropy of the income distribution (replace all the p_is with s_is in the above formula) from the maximum possible value of this entropy (when each $s_i = 1/n$, everyone gets an even share) we find the following contender for status as an inequality measure.

$$T = \sum_{i=1}^{n} \frac{1}{n} \; h(\tfrac{1}{n}) - \sum_{i=1}^{n} s_i \; h(s_i), \tag{1}$$

$$= \sum_{i=1}^{n} s_i [\, h(\tfrac{1}{n}) - h(s_i)\,], \tag{2}$$

$$= \sum_{i=1}^{n} s_i [\log s_i - \log(1/n)], \tag{3}$$

56

$$= \frac{1}{n} \sum_{i=1}^{n} \frac{y_i}{\overline{y}} \log(y_i/\overline{y}). \tag{4}$$

(Each of the expressions (1) to (4) is an equivalent way of
writing the measure T).

A diagrammatic representation of T can be found in
figure 3-4. In quadrant I, the function $\log(y/\overline{y})$ is plotted
(along the horizontal axis) against $y/\overline{y}$ (along the vertical
axis). In quadrant II we have the Parade (cf figure 2-1).
In quadrant III we have the Lorenz curve (upside down).
We use these three curves to derive the schedule in quadrant
IV. The method is as follows. Pick a particular value of F,
and find the corresponding value of $y/\overline{y}$ (i.e. find the height
of the man in the Parade after exactly $100.F\%$ of the Parade
has gone by). This determines the point Q_2 in quadrant II.
For this F-value, we can read off an equivalent Φ-value,
i.e. we find the proportion of the cake that has been handed
out by the time we reach the man with height $y/\overline{y}$. This
determines point Q_3 in quadrant III. Also read off the '$-h$'
value corresponding to $y/\overline{y}$; we do this by fixing point Q_1
in quadrant I. The positions of Q_1 and Q_3 fix a point Q_4 in
quadrant IV. By repeating this for every other F-value, we
trace out a curve in quadrant IV (The reader who yet needs
to be convinced may care to try plotting another set of
Q_1 Q_2 Q_3 Q_4 points as an exercise). This curve charts the
'information function' against income shares. Unfortunately
the entire curve cannot be shown in the diagram since it
crosses the $O\Phi$ axis; we have indicated the way it then
behaves by the dotted extension to the curve. The measure
T is then simply the area trapped between this curve and
the $O\Phi$ axis - shown as a shaded area.

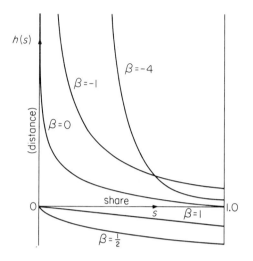

Figure 3-3

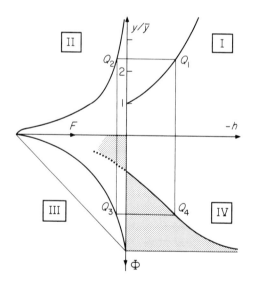

Figure 3-4

However this merely tells us about the mechanics of Theil's measure; we need to look more closely at its implications for the way we look at inequality. To do this, examine what happens to T if the share of a poor person ('man 1') is increased at the expense of a rich person ('man 2'). So let the share of man 1 increase from s_1 to a fractionally larger amount $s_1 + \Delta s$ and the share of 2 decrease to $s_2 - \Delta s$. Then, remembering that $h(s) = - \log s$, we find (by differentiation) that the resulting change in T is

$$\Delta T = \Delta s[h(s_2) - h(s_1)]$$

$$= - \Delta s \, \log(s_2/s_1).$$

As we would expect, the proposed transfer Δs results in a negative ΔT, so that the inequality index decreases. But we can say a little more than that. We see that the *size* of the reduction in T depends only on the ratio of s_2 to s_1. So for any two people with income shares in the same ratio, the transfer Δs (as above) would lead to the same reduction in inequality ΔT. Thus, for example, a small transfer from a person with an income share of 2 millionths, to a man with only 1 millionth of the cake has the same effect on Theil-inequality as an identical transfer from a man with 8 millionths of the national cake to one with 4 millionths.

This aids us to complete our analogy between inequality measurement and information theory. It is easy to see that income shares (s_i) serve as counterparts to probabilities (p_i). And now we can interpret the 'social analogue' of the information function h. Evidently from the formula for ΔT, we can now say under what circumstances s_3 and s_4 are the same 'distance apart' as s_2 and s_1. This would occur if $h(s_1) - h(s_2) = h(s_3) - h(s_4)$: a small transfer from s_2 to to s_1 has exactly the same effect on inequality as a small transfer from s_4 to s_3. Given this interpretation of $h(s)$ in terms of distance, do we want it to have *exactly* the same properties as $h(p)$ in information theory? There does not seem to be a compelling *a priori* reason why we should do so [we recall that the log-function was chosen in information theory so that $h(p_1 p_2) = h(p_1) + h(p_2)$], although $h(s) = -\log s$ gives us a reasonably sensible inequality measure, T. The function $(-\log s)$ can be seen as a member of a much wider class of functions, illustrated in figure 3-3. This figure charts members of the family of curves given by $h(s) = -\frac{1}{\beta} s^{\beta}$. Deriving an inequality measure in exactly the same way as before gives us, for any value of β that we choose, a particular inequality measure which may be written in any of the following ways:

$$I_\beta = \frac{1}{1+\beta} \left[\sum_{i=1}^{n} \frac{1}{n} \, h(\tfrac{1}{n}) - \sum_{i=1}^{n} s_i h(s_i) \right], \tag{5}$$

$$= \frac{1}{1+\beta} \sum_{i=1}^{n} s_i \left[h(\tfrac{1}{n}) - h(s_i) \right], \tag{6}$$

$$= \frac{1}{\beta + \beta^2} \left[\sum_{i=1}^{n} s_i^{\beta+1} - n^{-\beta} \right]. \tag{7}$$

And of course the effect of a small transfer Δs from rich man 2 to poor man 1 is now

$$\Delta I_\beta = -\frac{1}{\beta} \left[s_2^{\beta} - s_1^{\beta} \right] \Delta s$$

$$= \left[h(s_2) - h(s_1) \right] \Delta s$$

You get the same effect by transferring Δs from rich man 4

60

to poor man 3 if and only if the 'distance' $h(s_4) - h(s_3)$
is the same as the 'distance' $h(s_2) - h(s_1)$.

The special case I_0 (that is, where $\beta = 0$) is simply the
measure T. As we noted, this implies a *relative* concept of
distance: 1 and 2 are the same distance apart as 3 and 4 if
the ratios s_1/s_2 and s_3/s_4 are equal. Another interesting
special case is found by setting $\beta = 1$. Then

$$I_1 = \tfrac{1}{2}\left[\sum_{i=1}^{n} s_i^{\,2} - 1/n\right].$$

Now *Herfindahl's index* is simply

$$H = \sum_{i=1}^{n} s_i^{\,2} \; ;$$

that is, the sum of the squares of the income shares, so
that for a given population, I_1 and H are cardinally
equivalent. And in this case we have the very simple
absolute distance measure $h(s_1) - h(s_2) = s_1 - s_2$. Thus the
distance between a man with a 1% share and a man with a 2%
share is considered to be the same as the distance between
a man with a 4% share and a man with a 5% share.

So by choosing an appropriate 'distance function', we
determine a particular 'information theoretic' inequality
measure. In principle we can do this for an value of β.
Pick a particular curve in figure 3-3. The 'distance'
between any two income shares on the horizontal axis is
given by the linear distance between their two corresponding
points on the vertical axis. The β-curve of our choice
(suitably rotated) can then be plugged into quadrant I of
figure 3-4, and we thus derive a new curve in quadrant IV,

and obtain the inequality measure I_β. Notice the obvious
formal similarity between choosing one of the curves in
figure 3-3 and choosing a social utility function or welfare
index in figure 3-1a. If we write $\beta = -\varepsilon$, the analogy
appears to be almost complete: the choice of 'distance
function' seems to be determined simply by our relative
inequality aversion. Yet the approach of this section leads
to inequality measures that are somewhat different from
those found previously. The principal difference concerns
the inequality measures when $\beta \gtrless 0$. As we have seen I_β is
defined for such values. However, A_ε and D_ε become trivial
when ε is zero (since A_0 and D_0 are zero whatever the income
distribution); and usually neither A_ε nor D_ε is defined for
$\varepsilon < 0$ (corresponding to $\beta > 0$). Furthermore it is evident
that even for positive values of ε where I_β ranks any set
of income distributions in the same order as A_ε, A_ε and
I_ε are not cardinally equivalent. Which forms of inequality
measure should we choose then? The next section deals more
fully with this issue.

THE CHOICE OF INEQUALITY MEASURE

What we shall now do is consider more formally the
criteria we want satisfied by inequality measures. You may
be demanding why this has not been done before. The reason
is that I have been anxious to trace the origins of inequality measures already in use and to examine the assumptions
required at these origins. Had we wished, we could have
begun by specifying certain criteria in advance and then
from these derive the inequality measure or measures, but
this is a considerably harder task. However, now that we
have looked at *ad hoc* measures, and seen how the SWF and
information theory approaches work, we can collect our

thoughts on the properties of these measures. The importance of this exercise lies not only in the drawing up of
a shortlist of inequality measures by eliminating those
that are 'unsuitable'. It also helps to put personal
preference in perspective when choosing among those cited
in the shortlist. The criteria are italicised in the
following paragraphs.

Income Scale Independence   This means that measured
inequality should not depend on the size of the cake. If
everyone's income changes by the same proportion then it can
be argued that there has been no essential alteration in
the income distribution, and thus that the value of the
inequality measure should remain the same. This property is
possessed by all the inequality measures we have examined,
with the exception of the variance V, and Dalton's measure
with parameter zero, $D_0 = 1 - \log y^*/\log \bar{y}$. This is immediately
obvious in the case of those measures defined with respect
to income shares s_i, since a proportional income change in
all incomes leaves the shares unchanged.

Principle of Population   This requires that inequality
should not depend on the number of cake-receivers. If we
measure inequality in a particular economy with n people in
it and now merge the economy with another *identical* one,
we get a combined economy with a population of $2n$, and with
the same proportion of the population receiving any given
income. If measured inequality is the same for any such
replication of the economy, then the inequality measure
satisfies the principle of population. It is not self-
evident that this property is desirable. Consider a two-
person world where one man has all the income, and the
other has none. Then replicate the economy as just

explained, so that one now has a four-person world with two destitute people and two sharing income equally. It seems to me debatable whether these two worlds are 'equally unequal'. In fact nearly all the inequality measures we have considered *would* indicate this, since they satisfy the principle of population. The notable exception is I_β for $\beta \neq 0$; as the population is increased, I_β decreases for $\beta > 0$ (including Herfindahl's index of course), and increases for $\beta < 0$.

Weak Principle of Transfers In Chapter 2 we were interested to note whether each of the various inequality measures discussed there had the property that a hypothetical transfer of income from a rich man to a poor man reduces measured inequality. This property may now be stated more precisely. We shall say that an inequality measure satisfies the weak principle of transfers if the following is always true. Consider any two individuals, one with income y, the other, a richer man, with income $y + \delta$ where δ is positive. Then transfer a positive amount of income Δy from the richer to the poorer man, where Δy is less than $\frac{1}{2}\delta$. Inequality should then definitely decrease. If this property is true for some inequality measure, no matter what values of y and $y + \delta$ we use, then we may use the following theorem.

THEOREM 2 Suppose the distribution of income in social state B could be achieved by a simple redistribution of income in social state A (i.e. total income is the same in each case), and that the Lorenz curve for B lies wholly inside that of A. Then, as long as an inequality measure satisfies the weak principle of transfers, that inequality measure will *always* indicate a strictly lower level of inequality for state B than for state A.

This result is not exactly surprising, because it is evident that by our interpretation of the Lorenz curve in Chapter 2 we could get to state B from state A by a series of rich-to-poor transfers of the type mentioned above. However, it emphasises the importance of this 'principle' for choosing between inequality measures. As we have seen in these two chapters, V, c, G, T, H, A_ε, D_ε ($\varepsilon > 0$) and I_β all pass this test; v and v_1 fail the test in the case of high incomes – it is possible for these to rank A as superior to B. The other measures, R, M, the equal shares coefficient, etc, *just* fail the test – in the case of these measures it would be possible for state B's Lorenz curve to lie partly 'inside' and to lie nowhere 'outside' that of state A, and yet exhibit no reduction in measured inequality. In other words, we have achieved a situation where there has been *some* redistribution from rich to poor, but no change in inequality occurs. I have qualified the definition given above as the *weak* principle of transfers, because all that it requires is that given the specified transfer, inequality should decrease. But it says nothing about *how much* it should decrease. To examine this issue more carefully, consider the next property.

Strong Principle of Transfers Once we introduce the notion of 'distance' between people we can, if we like, strengthen the principle of transfers. For example, take a distance measure $d = h(s_1) - h(s_2)$, where s_2 is greater than s_1, and $h(s)$ is one of the curves in figure 3-3. Then consider a transfer from rich man 2 to poor man 1. We say that the inequality measure satisfies the principle of transfers in the *strong* sense if the *amount* of the reduction in inequality depends only on d, the distance, no matter which two individuals we choose. For the kind of h-functions illustrated in figure 3-3, the inequality measures that satisfy this strong principle of transfers belong to the family described by formula (6) for I_β, of which the Theil index and the Herfindahl index are special cases. Each value of β defines a different concept of distance, and thus a different associated inequality measure satisfying the strong principle of transfers.

Why should we want to strengthen the principle of transfers in this way? One obvious reason is that merely requiring that a measure satisfies the weak principle gives us so much latitude that we cannot even find a method of ranking all possible income distributions in an unambiguous order. This is because, as theorem 2 shows, the weak principle amounts to a requirement that the measure should rank income distributions in the same fashion as the associated Lorenz curves - no more, no less. Now the strong principle of transfers *by itself* does not give this guidance, but it points the way to an intuitively appealing method. Several writers have noted that an inequality measure incorporates some sort of average of income differences. The 'distance' concept, d, allows one to formalise this. For, given a particular d, one may derive a unique inequality measure by using the strong principle as a fundamental axiom[†]. This measure takes the form of the average distance between each person's actual income and the income he would receive in a perfectly equal society, and includes I_β - see formula (6). The advantage of this is that instead of postulating the existence of a SWF, discussing its

---

† For the other axioms required see Cowell and Kuga (1976).

desired properties, and then deriving the measure, one may
discuss the basic idea of distance between income shares
then derive the inequality measure directly.

Many, though not all, of such measures will be *ordinally*
equivalent to inequality measures arising naturally from
the SWF method. We have already emphasised this equivalence
in the case of I_β and A_ε, for $\beta = -\varepsilon$ where ε is positive.
If all one is concerned with is the ordering property of
the measures, then the key decision is *which* distance con-
cept (value of β) or *which value* of inequality aversion (ε)
should be chosen. This choice determines how the 'tie' will
be broken in cases where two Lorenz curves intersect – the
problem mentioned in Chapter 2. This point is illustrated
in figure 3-5. For low values of ε, the distribution marked
B is regarded as 'less unequal' than distribution C; for
high values of ε, and the related concepts of distance,
the position is exactly reversed. The value of β or ε that
is chosen depends on two things: (a) one's intrinsic
aversion to inequality; (b) the discriminatory power of the

ε	A_ε	
	B	C
	(1973/4)	(1957)
0.1	0.024	0.025
0.5	0.112	0.109
1.0	0.207	0.193

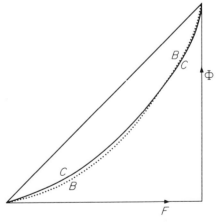

Source: *National Income and Expenditure*, UK income before tax

Figure 3-5

resulting inequality measure. Point (a) is just a restate-
ment of our earlier discussion relating ε to our willing-
ness to sacrifice overall income in order to pursue an
egalitarian redistribution; a more practical example occurs
in Chapter 5. The detail covering point (b) has to be
deferred to Chapter 5; however, the main point is that if
very high inequality aversion is specified, nearly all
income distributions that are encountered will register high
measured inequality, so that it becomes difficult to say
whether one state is more unequal than another.

Most of the *ad hoc* inequality measures do not satisfy
the strong principle of transfers as they stand, although
many are ordinally equivalent to measures satisfying this
axiom. In such cases, the size of a change in inequality due
to an income transfer depends not only on the distance
between the shares of the persons concerned, but on the
measured value of overall inequality as well. It is interesting to note the distance concept implied by these
measures. Implicit in the use of the variance and the coefficient of variation (which are ordinally equivalent to
H) is the notion that distance equals the absolute difference between income shares. The relative mean deviation
implies a very odd notion of distance - zero if both men are
on the same side of the mean, and one if they are on
opposite sides. This property can be deduced from the effect
of the particular redistribution illustrated in figure 2-5.
The measures v, v_1 and G are not even ordinally equivalent
to a measure satisfying the strong principle. In the case of
v and v_1 this is because they do not satisfy the weak
principle either; the reason for G's failure is more subtle.
Here the size of the change in inequality arising from a
redistribution between two people depends on their relative

location in the Parade, *not* on the absolute size of their
incomes or their income shares. Hence a redistribution
from the 4th to the 5th person (arranged in parade order)
has the same effect as a transfer from the 1,000,004th to
the 1,000,005th, whatever their respective incomes. So
distance cannot be defined in terms of the individual
income shares alone.

A further reason for recommending the strong principle
lies in the cardinal properties of inequality measures. In
much of the literature attention is focused on ordinal
properties, and rightly so. However, sometimes this has
meant that because any transformation of an inequality
measure leaves its ordering properties unchanged, cardinal
characteristics have been neglected or rather arbitrarily
specified. For example, it is often recommended that the
inequality measure should be normalised so that it always
lies between zero and one. To use this as a recommendation
for a particular ordinally equivalent variant of the inequality measure is dubious for three reasons. (1) It is
not clear that a finite maximum value of inequality,
independent of the number in the population, is desirable.
(2) There are many ways of transforming the measure such
that it lies in the zero-to-one range, each such transformation having different cardinal properties. In particular, (3) where the untransformed measure has a finite
maximum, the measure can easily be normalised *without*
altering its cardinal properties simply by dividing by that
maximum value.[†]

However, because measures satisfying the strong
principle of transfers can be written down as the sum of a

† This assumes that the minimum value is zero; but the
required normalisation is easy whatever the minimum value.

function of each income share, they have attractive
cardinal properties when one considers either the decomposition of inequality within constituent parts of the
population, or changes in measured inequality. In fact, the
family I_β (all of which satisfy the strong principle) may be
written in such a way that changes in inequality overall
can easily be related to (i) changes in inequality *within*
given subgroups of the population, and (ii) changes in the
income shares enjoyed by these subgroups, and hence the
inequality *between* the groups. The detail of this argument
is in the appendix, whence it is clear that a measure such
as A_ε, though formally ordinally equivalent to I_β for many
values of β, does not decompose nearly so easily. These
cardinal properties are, of course, very important when
one considers empirical applications, as we do in Chapter 5.

The upshot of the argument of Chapters 2 and 3, then,
is as follows. If one is interested in dealing with any and
every possible income distribution, the minimal requirement of the weak principle of transfers should be satisfied.
In choosing a measure that conforms to this principle it is
useful to have one that may either be related to an inequality-aversion parameter (such as A_ε or D_ε) or to a concept of distance between income shares (I_β). This still
leaves the question of various cardinal characteristics
open. Invariance with respect to proportional changes in
all incomes or with respect to increases in the population
may be desirable under certain circumstances. Standardisation
of the measure in a given range (such as 0 to 1) has only a
superficial attractiveness to recommend it: it may be well
worth while sacrificing this in order to put the measure
in a cardinal form more useful for analysing the composition of, and changes in, inequality. The way these

conclusions relate to the measures we have mentioned is summarised in table 3-1.

However, these remarks apply to comparisons of all conceivable distributions. You may wonder whether our task can be made easier if our attention is restricted to those distributions that in some sense are likely to arise. The next chapter attempts to deal with this issue.

Table 3-1

Name	Principle of Transfers †	Distance concept	Independent of proportional increases in incomes and in population?	Range in interval [0,1]?
Variance (V)	SPT	Absolute differences	No: increases	No: unbounded above
Coefficient of variation (c)	WPT	As for variance	Yes	No: unbounded above
Relative mean deviation (M)	just fails	Distance is zero between income shares on the same side of the mean, unity between income shares on opposite sides of the mean	Yes	Yes: if the measure is multiplied by $\frac{1}{2}$
Logarithmic variance (v)	fails	Differences in logarithms of incomes divided by the incomes themselves	Yes	No: unbounded above
Variance of logarithms (v_1)	fails	As for logarithmic variance	Yes	No: unbounded above
Equal shares coefficient	just fails	As for relative mean deviation	Yes	Yes

Minimal majority	just fails	Similar to relative mean deviation (critical income is not the arithmetic mean, but y_Q, defined on page and in the appendix)	Yes	Yes
Gini (G)	WPT	Depends on *rank order* of individuals in the population	Yes	Yes
Atkinson's index (A_ε)	WPT	Difference in marginal social utilities	Yes	Yes
Dalton's index (D_ε)	SPT	As for Atkinson's index	Yes *except for $\varepsilon=1$*	Yes: for $\varepsilon \neq 1$
Theil's entropy index (T)	SPT	Proportional differences	Yes	No: unbounded above
Herfindahl's index (H)	SPT	As for variance	No: decreases with population size	Yes: but minimum value is greater than zero

† SPT = strong principle of transfers; WPT = weak principle of transfers; fails = fails to satisfy even WPT. Notice that the relative mean deviation, equal shares, and minimal majority coefficients only just fail this test in that a transfer from rich to poor may leave measured inequality unchanged rather than reducing it.

4
Important special cases

'I distrust all systematisers and avoid them.
The will to a system shows a lack of honesty'

- F.W. Nietzsche (1888),
Maxims and Missiles.

In this chapter we shall meet some more specialised jargon,
and so it is probably a good idea at the outset to consider
in general terms why it is worth while becoming acquainted
with this new terminology. The special cases which we shall
examine consist of situations in which it is convenient or
reasonable to make use of a mathematical formula that
approximates the distribution (or part of the distribution)
in which we are interested. The inconvenience of having to
acquaint oneself with a specific formulation is usually
compensated for by a simplification of the problem of
comparing distributions in different populations, or of
examining the evolution of a distribution over time.

At the outset it is necessary to understand the concept
of a *functional form*. Typically this is a mathematical
formula which defines the distribution function (or the
density function, depending on the particular presentation)
of not just a single distribution, but of a whole family of

such distributions. Each family member has common characteristics and can usually be simply identified within the family by fixing certain numbers known as *parameters*. This can be clarified by an easy example that may be very familiar. Consider the family of all the straight lines that can be drawn on a simple plane diagram. The usual equation that gives the graph of the straight line is:

$y = mx + c,$

where y is distance in the 'vertical' direction and x is distance in the 'horizontal' direction. Since this formula defines *any* straight line in the plane, it can be considered as a general description of the whole family – i.e. as the functional form referred to above. The numbers m and c are, in this case, the parameters. Fix them and you fix a particular straight line as a family member. For example, if you put $m=1$ and $c=2$ you get a line with slope 1 (or, a 45-degree line) that has an intercept on the y-axis at $y=2$.

When we are dealing with functional forms that are useful in the analysis of inequality, however, we are not of course immediately interested in straight lines, but rather in curves which will look like figures 2–2a or 2–2b. In this case our parameters usually fix things such as the *location* of the distribution (for example, if one of the parameters is the arithmetic mean) and the *dispersion* of the distribution (for example, if one of the parameters is the variance).

Now perhaps it is possible to see the advantage of adopting a particular functional form. Let us suppose that you have discovered a formula that fits a particular distribution superbly. We will write down the density function of your fitted formula thus:

$$f = \phi(y\,;\,a,b).$$

The notation $\phi(.\,;.\,,.)$ simply stands for some expression the details of which we have not troubled to specify; a and b are the parameters. This equation gives you the height f of the smooth curve in figure 2-2a for any value of income y. Obviously a and b have particular numerical values which give a close fit to the distribution you are examining. However, the empirical distribution that you are considering may be of a very common shape, and it may so happen that your formula will also do for the distribution of income in another population. Then all you have to do is to specify new values of a and b in order to fix a new member of the ϕ-family. And so you could go on using your formula again and again for different distributions (assuming it *was* a good approximation of course!), each time merely having to reset the two numbers a and b. So, let us suppose that the problem in hand is the comparison of the distribution of income in a particular country now with what is was ten years ago, and that it turns out that in each case the ϕ-formula you have discovered very closely fits the observed shape. The comparison is really very easy because you do not have to describe the whole distribution, but *you can neatly summarise the whole change by noting the change in the two numbers a and b.* No more is required because in specifying a and b you have thus described the whole curve, in the same way that 'slope' and 'intercept' completely describe an entire straight line.

Because this approach is so convenient it is appropriate to put in some words of warning before going any further. Although this chapter only discusses two functional forms in detail, a great many others have been employed in the social sciences. The properties of some of these are described in the appendix. However, any such formula is only a convenience. It may turn out that it describes some distributions extremely well, but this should not lull us into expecting it to perform miracles in every situation. Most often we find that such a functional form characterises certain sections of a distribution. In this case we need to be very aware of its limitations in the less convenient parts – frequently these are the 'lower tail' of the distribution. It is usually only fortuitous that a very simple formula turns out to be a highly satisfactory description of the facts in every respect. Finally, in the analysis of economic inequality it is often the case that a simple theoretical caricature of the income- or wealth-generating process leads one to anticipate in theory that a particular functional form of the income or wealth distribution may be realised. Such a conclusion, of course, can only be as sound as the assumptions of the model underlying it. Therefore one is well advised to be suspicious about 'laws' of distribution in the sense of claiming that a particular formulation is *the* one that is somehow metaphysically 'correct'. In doing so it may be possible to view such formulations in what I believe is the correct perspective – as useful approximations that enable us to describe a lot about different distributions with a minimum of effort.

THE LOGNORMAL DISTRIBUTION

In order to grasp the reason for using this apparently unusual distribution with a complicated density function (the mathematical specification is given in the appendix) it is helpful to come to an understanding of its historical and logical origin. This requires a preliminary consideration of the normal distribution.

The normal distribution itself is of fundamental importance in a vast area of applied statistics, and for an appreciation of its origin and significance reference should be made to sources cited in the notes to this chapter. For our present purposes let us note that since 'the normal curve was, in fact, to the early statisticians what the circle was to the Ptolemaic astronomers'[†] it is not surprising that scholars have been eager to press it into service in the field of economics and elsewhere. If examination marks, men's height, and errors in experimental observation[¶] were supposed to have the normal distribution, then why not look for a 'normal law' governing the distribution of observed quantities in the social sciences?

The term 'normal distribution' describes one family of possible frequency curves, two typical members of which are illustrated in figure 4-1. As you can see, the curves are symmetrical about the line $A'A$; A marks the value μ which is the arithmetic mean of the variable x whose distribution is described by curve (1). This is also the mean of a variable with the distribution of curve (2), which by construction has been drawn with the same mid-value. If curve (2) had a higher mean then it would be displaced bodily to the right of its present position. The higher the variance of the distribution, σ^2, the more 'spread out'

---

† Yule and Kendall (1950).

¶ It has now long been recognised that the distributions of many such observed characteristics only rarely approximate very closely to the normal distribution. This in no way diminishes the importance of the normal in sampling theory, nor in understanding the historical origin of much of the thought concerning the distribution of incomes.

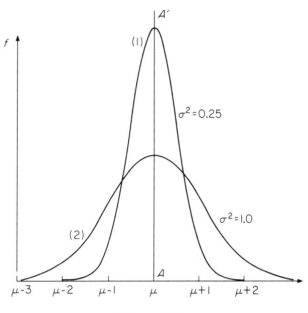

Figure 4-1

will this curve be – compare the values of σ^2 for the two curves. The two numbers μ, σ^2 are the curves' parameters and so completely identify a particular member of the family of normal distributions. If a particular variable x (such as height in a sample of adult males) has the normal distribution with mean μ and variance σ^2, we say that x is distributed $N(x; \mu, \sigma^2)$.

Now it is evident that the distribution of economic quantities such as income does not fit the normal curve (although there are some latter day Ptolemaians who would like to assure us that they 'really' do – see, for example, Lebergott, 1959). As we have seen in Chapter 2, typical income distributions are positively skewed, with a long right-hand tail – this is even more noticeable in the case

of the distribution of wealth. Is there a simple
theoretical distribution that captures this feature?

The lognormal distribution has been suggested as such a
candidate, and may be explained in the following manner.
Suppose we are considering the distribution of a variable
y (income) and we find that the *logarithm* of y has the
normal distribution, then y is said to be lognormally
distributed. So if we transform all our y-values to
x-values thus:

$x = \log y$,

(the shape of the curve that describes the relation is
given by the $\varepsilon=1$ curve in figure 3-1a), we will find that
has the normal distribution like the curves in figure 4-1.
But what does the distribution of the untransformed
variable y itself look like? Two representative members of
the lognormal family are illustrated in figure 4-2.

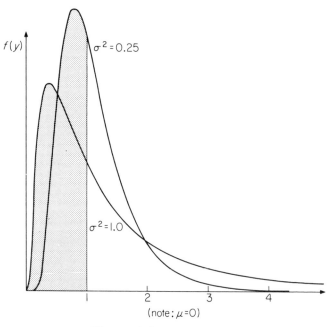

Figure 4-2

Notice that, unlike the normal distribution, it is not defined for negative values of the variable y. The reason for this is that as x (the logarithm of y) becomes large and negative, y itself approaches its minimum value of zero, and there is no real number x representing the logarithm of a negative number.

However, the perceptive reader may by now be asking himself, why choose a logarithmic transformation to produce a distribution of the 'right' shape? There are four reasons. Firstly, the lognormal distribution has a lot of convenient properties, some of which are explained below. Secondly, it can be shown that under certain kinds of 'random processes' the distribution of incomes eventually turns out to be approximately lognormal. The idea here, roughly speaking, is that the changes in people's incomes can be likened to a systematic process whereby, in each moment of time, a person's income increases or decreases by a certain proportion, the exact proportionate increase being determined by chance. If the distribution of these proportionate increments or decrements follows the normal law, then in many cases the overall distribution of income approaches lognormality, provided that you allow enough time for the process to operate.[†] Thirdly, there is still some residual notion of 'individual utility' or 'social welfare' associated with the logarithm of income; it would be nice to claim that although incomes do not follow the normal distribution, 'utility' or 'welfare' does. This will

---

† Of course, other technical assumptions are required to ensure convergence to the lognormal. In some cases the resulting distribution is similar to, but not exactly equivalent to, the lognormal. This kind of process is also very useful in analysing the inequality in the size distribution of firms.

not do, however, for as we have seen in Chapter 3, even if
we do introduce a SWF, log y is just one among many
candidate 'welfare indices'.[†] Fourthly, the lognormal
provides a reasonable sort of fit to many actual sets of
data. This I shall consider later.

Our first reason for using the logarithmic
transformation of the normal distribution was, unashamedly,
the convenient properties which the resulting distribution
possessed. I shall now display these a little more boldly.

THE LOGNORMAL - SPECIAL ATTRACTIONS

*** A simple relationship to the normal curve for
which tables are readily available.

*** Symmetrical Lorenz curves.

*** Non-intersecting Lorenz curves.

*** Easy interpretation of parameters.

*** Preservation under log-linear transformations.

Let us look more closely at the 'small print' behind
these claims. The first point, on the relationship with the
normal curve we have already examined in detail. However,
it is worth noting that this simple transformation enables
the student very easily to look up the cumulative frequency
$F(y)$ corresponding to an income y (the proportion of the
population with an income no greater than y): look up the
logarithm of y, say x; 'standardise' this number using the
two parameters to calculate $z = [x-\mu]/\sigma$; look up $F(z)$ in

---

† Incidentally, Champernowne's (1953, 1973) use of the term
  'income power' to describe log y is blameless on this
  score. This is simply a matter of terminological
  convenience so that he can look at income *proportions*
  rather than incomes themselves.

the tables of the standard normal distribution. A further advantage of this close relationship is that a number of common statistical tests which rely on the assumption of normality can be applied straightaway to the logarithm of income, given the lognormal assumption.

The second feature, the symmetry of Lorenz curves, was noted by Aitchison and Brown (1954), and is illustrated by figure 4-3. The axis of symmetry is obviously the line which intersects the typical Lorenz curve where y attains its mean value at the point P. This is a little more than a theoretical curiosity since it enables the student to see quickly whether there is a *prima facie* case for using the lognormal as an approximation to some given set of data. If the plotted Lorenz curve does not look symmetrical, then it is not very likely that the lognormality assumption will turn out to be satisfactory. The third feature, non-intersecting Lorenz curves, can also be seen in figure 4-3.[†] The important conclusion to be derived from this observation is this: *given any two members of the lognormal family of distributions, one will unambiguously exhibit greater inequality than the other*. This remark is to be understood in the sense of comparing the inequality exhibited by the two income distributions using any mean-independent inequality measure that satisfies the principle of transfers. It is a direct consequence of theorem 1 in the last chapter, and it is an observation which leads us naturally on to the next feature.

The fourth feature is well-documented. Since there is a simple link with the normal, we may expect a simple link

---

† It should be noted that this does *not* follow from the second property. Two arbitrary Lorenz curves, each of which is symmetric, may of course intersect.

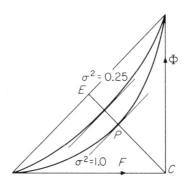

Figure 4-3

between the parameters μ, σ^2 of the lognormal distribution, written $\Lambda(y; \mu, \sigma^2)$, and the normal distribution. It is evident by definition that μ is the mean of the logarithm of y (or, putting the same point another way, μ is the logarithm of the geometric mean of the values of y). It also happens that μ is the logarithm of the median of y – so that 50% of the distribution lies to the left of the value $y = e^{\mu}$ – see the shaded area in figure 4-2. Again by definition we see that σ^2 is the variance of the logarithm of y; this is the inequality measure we denoted by v_1 in Chapter 2. As we noted in the last paragraph, if we are comparing members of the two-parameter lognormal family, we never have the problem of intersecting Lorenz curves.[†] Furthermore, since any Lorenz curve is defined independently of the mean, it

---

[†] The problem can arise if one considers more complicated versions of the lognormal curve, such as the three-parameter variant, or if one examines observations from a lognormal population that has been truncated or censored. Consideration of these points is an unnecessary detour in our argument; reference may be made to Aitchison and Brown (1957).

can be shown that the family of Lorenz curves corresponding to the family of lognormal distributions is independent of the parameter μ. Thus each lognormal Lorenz curve is uniquely labelled by the parameter σ^2. So σ (or σ^2) itself is a satisfactory inequality measure, provided that we restrict our attention to the lognormal family. Of course, if we go outside the family we may encounter the problems noted on page 31. However, although σ or σ^2 may perform the task of ordinally ranking lognormal curves perfectly well, we may not be attracted by its cardinal properties. Just because the variance of logarithms, σ^2, is a convenient parameter of the lognormal distribution we do not have to use it as an inequality measure. Fortunately, it is very easy to express other inequality measures as simple functions of σ, and a table giving the formula for these is to be found in the appendix. Some of those which were discussed in the last two chapters are sketched against the corresponding values of σ^2 in figure 4-4. Thus to find, say, the value of the Gini coefficient in a population with the lognormal distribution, locate the relevant value of σ^2 on the horizontal axis, and then read off the corresponding value of the inequality measure on the vertical axis from the curve marked Gini.

The final point may seem a little mystifying, though it can be useful. It follows in fact from a well-known property of the normal distribution: if a variable x is distributed $N(x;\mu,\sigma^2)$, then the simple transformation $z = a+bx$ has the distribution $N(z;a+b\mu,b^2\sigma^2)$, i.e. the transformed variable also has the normal distribution, but with mean and variance altered as shown. Let us see how this applies to the lognormal distribution. Now we know that a variable y has the lognormal distribution $\Lambda(y;\mu,\sigma^2)$ if its logarithm $x=\log y$

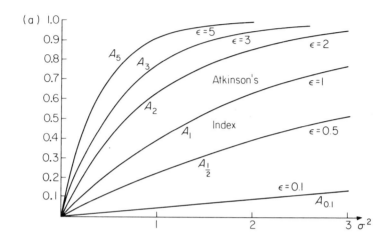

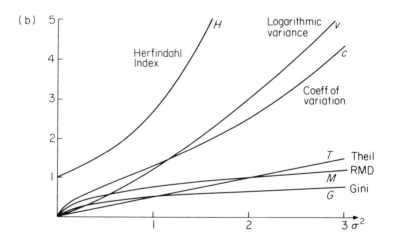

Figure 4-4

has the normal distribution $N(y;\mu, \sigma^2)$. Suppose we consider any two numbers A,b with the only restriction that A be positive, and write the natural logarithm of A as a. Use these two numbers to transform y into another variable thus: $w=Ay^b$, so that by the usual rule of taking logarithms we have $\log w = a+b \log y$. Denote $\log w$ by z and recall the definition that we made above of $x=\log y$. Then the last equation can be more simply written $z=a+bx$. But we know (from above) that because x is distributed $N(x;\mu,\sigma^2)$, z is distributed $N(z;a+b\mu,b^2\sigma^2)$. In other words, the logarithm of w has the normal distribution with mean $a+b\mu$, and variance $b^2\sigma^2$. By definition of the lognormal, therefore, w itself has the lognormal distribution $\Lambda(w;a+b\mu,b^2\sigma^2)$. To summarize: if y is distributed $\Lambda(y; \mu,\sigma^2)$, then the transformed variable $w=Ay^b$ has the distribution $\Lambda(w; a+b\mu,b^2\sigma^2)$. **One of the** useful applications of this property is as follows. It has been observed that many country's personal tax schedules are approximated by the formula $t= y-Ay^b$, where t is individual tax liability and y is income.[†] Then disposable income is given by $w=Ay^b$. So if the distribution of pre-tax income is approximately lognormal, the distribution of after-tax income is also approximately lognormal.

We will find some very similar properties when we turn to our second special case.

[†] A tax function with this property has been called a 'constant residual progression' tax function after the terminology used by Musgrave and Thin (1948). The parameter b lies between 0 and 1; the smaller is b, the more progressive is the tax schedule; and the smaller is the inequality in the resulting distribution of disposable income.

THE PARETO DISTRIBUTION

Although the Pareto formulation has proved to be
extremely versatile in the social sciences, in my view the
purpose for which it was originally employed is still its
most useful application – an approximate description of the
distribution of incomes among the rich and the moderately
rich. In the course of the examination of the upper tails
of the income distributions in a number of countries,
Pareto found a remarkably close fit to that particular two-
parameter distribution which now bears his name. Since the
functional form 'worked' not only for the then current
(late nineteenth century) data, but also for earlier
periods (as far back as the worthy citizens of Augsburg in
1471), this happy empirical circumstance assumed the status
of a law. Furthermore, since the value of the crucial
parameter (now customarily referred to as 'Pareto's α')
seemed to lie within a fairly narrow range, it seemed to
Pareto that α might receive the kind of dignification
accorded to the gravitational constant in physics.

Unfortunately, I must remind you of the iconoclastic
remarks about 'laws' made earlier in this chapter. Although
the Paretian functional form provides a good fit for parts
of many income or wealth distributions (as well as an
abundance of other engaging applications such as the size
distribution of cities, the frequency of contribution by
authors to learned journals, the frequency of words in the
Nootka and Plains Cree languages, the distribution of the
length of intervals between repetitions of notes in Mozart's
Bassoon Concerto in B♭ Major, and the ranking of the
billiards scores by faculty members of Indiana University),
the reputation accorded to it by earlier and more naive
interpretations has become somewhat tarnished. Neither

Davis' mathematical interpretation of history, nor
Bernadelli's postulate of the futility of revolutions is
comfortably supported by the facts on income distribution.[†]
But although the more simplistic hopes (centring on the
supposed constancy of Pareto's α) may have been dashed, the
underlying distribution remains of fundamental importance
for the following reasons.

In the first place, although Pareto's α is not a
gravitational constant, as I have pointed out, the
functional form still works well for a number of sets of
data. Secondly, the distribution may once again be shown to
be related to a simple 'random process' theory of
individual income development. The details of this are set
out in full in Champernowne (1953, 1973) and the nontechnical reader will find a simple summary in Pen (1971).
The principle is very similar to the process referred to on
page 81, the main difference being that a device is
introduced to prevent an indefinite increase in dispersion
over time, which as the effect of erecting a 'lower barrier'
income y below which noone can fall. Thirdly, the Paretian
form can be shown to result from simple hypotheses about the
formation of individual remuneration within bureaucratic
organisations. The works of Simon (1957) and Lydall (1968)
are examples. The idea here is quite simple: given that a
hierarchical salary structure exists and that there is a
fairly stable relationship between the remuneration of
overlord and underling, the resulting frequency distribution
of incomes is Paretian. Fourthly, the functional form of the
Pareto distribution has some remarkably convenient

---

† Curious readers are invited to check the notes to this
chapter for details.

properties in its own right which make it useful for a description of distributional problems and for some technical manipulations, which I discuss in the next chapter.

In order to understand the especially attractive feature of the Pareto distribution you will find it helpful to construct a fresh diagram to present the income distribution data. This will be based on the same facts as were figures 2-1 to 2-4 but will set out the information in a different manner. Along the horizontal axis put income on a logarithmic scale (i.e. a scale similar to that used in figure 2-4). On the vertical axis put cumulative income proportions $F(y)$ transformed in the following way. For any income level y calculate the number $P = 1-F(y)$; this gives you the proportion of the population with £y *or more*. Then plot P on a logarithmic scale also. Let us see what the resulting curve must look like. If we look at a low level of income, then the corresponding value of $F(y)$ will be low since there will only be a small proportion of the population with that income *or less*. By the same token the corresponding value of P must be relatively high (close to its maximum value of 1.0). If we look at a much higher level of y, $F(y)$ will be higher (the proportion of the population with that income or less will have risen) and, of course, the number P will be smaller (the proportion of the population with that income or more must have fallen). As we consider larger and larger values of y, the number P dwindles away to its minimum value of zero. Since P is being plotted on a logarithmic scale (and the logarithm of zero is minus infinity) this means that the right-hand end of the curve must go right off the bottom edge of the page. The result is a picture like that

90

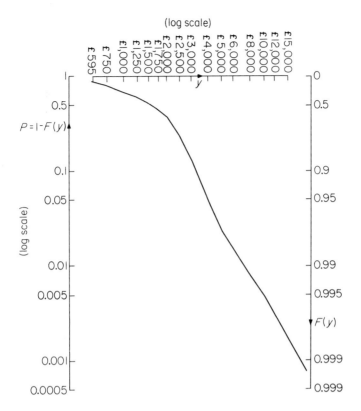

Source: as for figure 2-1.

Figure 4-5

of figure 4-5. Notice that part of this curve looks as though it may be satisfactorily approximated by a straight line with slope of about $-2\frac{1}{2}$. This gives us the clue to the Pareto distribution.

If the graph we have just drawn turns out to be exactly a straight line throughout its length, then the underlying distribution is known as the Pareto distribution. The slope of the line (taken positively) is one of the parameters of the distribution, usually denoted by α. The income

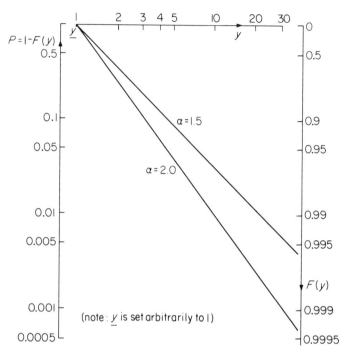

Figure 4-6

corresponding to the intercept of the line on the
horizontal axis gives the other parameter; write this as $\underline{y}$.
Two examples of the Pareto family, each with the same $\underline{y}$, but
with different values of α are illustrated in figure 4-6.
The corresponding frequency distributions are drawn in
figure 4-7. It is apparent from a superficial comparison of
this picture with figure 2-2a or other frequency
distributions based on different data sets that, for income
distributions at least, the Paretian functional form is not
likely to be a very good fit in the lower and middle income

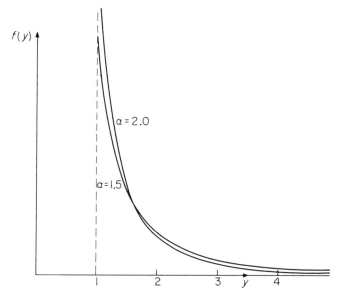

Figure 4-7.

classes but may turn out to be a good fit in the upper ranges, as suggested at the beginning of the section. We shall consider this further in the next section.

Let us, then, see what special attractions of the Pareto distribution might be advertised.

PARETO - SPECIAL ATTRACTIONS

***   Exact linearity of the Pareto diagram.

***   Van der Wijk's law.

***   Non-intersecting Lorenz curves.

***   Easy interpretation of parameters.

***   Preservation under loglinear transformations.

Once again we ought to look at the facts behind these assertions. The first point, the linearity of the Pareto diagram, has already been brought out in detail above. One particular advantage of this, however, is that because of this simple shape it is easy to work out the distribution function $F(y)$, i.e. to calculate the proportion of the population that has £y or less. To do this, divide $\underline{y}$ by the required income level y; raise the resulting number to the power α; subtract this result from 1.

On the second point, we find van der Wijk's name attached to a particularly simple law which holds only for the Pareto distribution.[†] Take any income level y. Then the average income of everyone who gets £y or more is simply $\frac{\alpha}{\alpha-1} y$, i.e. there is a simple proportionality relationship between this average and the chosen income level, whatever the value of y. Notice that if α increases, the gap between your income of £y, say, and the average income of everyone else above you, namely £ $\frac{\alpha}{\alpha-1} y$, necessarily gets smaller: if $\alpha = 1.5$, then those above you have an average income three times your own; if $\alpha = 2$, then those above you have an average income only twice that which you receive.

The third assertion (of non-intersecting Lorenz curves) is illustrated in figure 4-8, and can be readily inferred from the explicit formula for the Lorenz curve of the Pareto distribution given in the appendix. From that formula it may be seen that if we choose any value of F in figure 4-8 (measured along the horizontal axis), then as we choose

---

† This is true for all *continuous* distributions. There is a distribution defined for discrete variables (where y takes positive integer values only) which also satisfies the law. See the appendix.

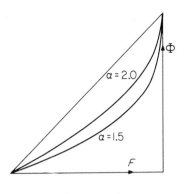

Figure 4-8

successively larger values of α, each lying on a new
Lorenz curve, the corresponding value of Φ must become prog-
ressively larger. In other words, as we choose larger
values of α *all* the points on the relevant Lorenz curve must
lie closer to the diagonal. So no two Paretian Lorenz curves
can cross.

These observations take us naturally on to our fourth
point - the interpretation of the parameters. You may already
have come to suspect that the parameter α reveals something
about the amount of inequality exhibited by a particular
Pareto distribution. Since it is evident that, within the
Pareto family, Lorenz curves associated with higher values of
α are closer to the line of perfect equality, it follows that
if we compare two Pareto distributions with the same mean,
the one with the higher value of α exhibits the *less* amount
of inequality for all inequality measures satisfying the
principle of transfers.[†]

[†] An intuitive argument can be employed here. Using van der
Wijk's law you find that the gap between your own income
and the average income of everyone above you diminishes
the larger is α. Thus the 'unfairness' of the income
distribution as perceived by you has diminished.

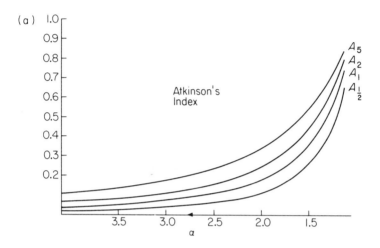

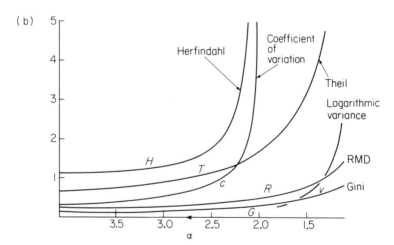

Figure 4-9

Once again, just because the parameter α is convenient in
the case of the Pareto distribution, this does not mean that
there is any particular merit in using it as a measure of
equality. We may prefer the cardinal characteristics of some
other measure, in which case we may compute the alternative
measure as a function of α using the table in the appendix,
or using figure 4-9. This figure is to be interpreted in a
manner very similar to that of figure 4-4 in the case of the
lognormal distribution. The interpretation of the parameter
$\underline{y}$ can easily be seen from figure 4-7, which as been drawn
with $\underline{y}$ set arbitrarily to one. This parameter may assume any
positive (but *not* zero) value, and gives the lower income
limit for which the distribution is defined. By a simple
application of van der Wijk's law, putting yourself at
minimum income $\underline{y}$, it can be seen that mean income for the
whole population is $\frac{\alpha}{\alpha-1} \underline{y}$. So average income is proportional to minimum income, and is a decreasing function of α.[†]

The formal meaning of the fifth and final point in our
list is the same as in the case of the lognormal

[†] Another apparently paradoxical result needs to be included
for completeness here. Specify any social welfare function
that satisfies properties 1 to 3 of Chapter 3 (note that
we are not even insisting on concavity of the SWF). Then
consider a change from one Pareto distribution to another
Pareto distribution with a higher α but the same value of
minimum income $\underline{y}$ (for example the two curves in figure
4-7). We find that social welfare decreases with α,
although, as we have seen, inequality also decreases for
any 'sensible' mean-independent inequality measure. Why
does this occur? It is simply that as α is increased ($\underline{y}$
held constant) mean income, $\bar{y} = \alpha \underline{y} / [\alpha-1]$ decreases, and
this decrease in average income is sufficient to wipe out
any favourable effect on social welfare from the reduction
in equality. Of course, if α is increased, *and* minimum
income $\underline{y}$ is increased so as to keep $\bar{y}$ constant, social
welfare is increased for any individualistic, additive
and concave social welfare function.

distribution. A proof is not difficult. Suppose that the quantity y has the Pareto distribution with parameters $\underline{y}$ and α. Then from the appendix we find that the proportion of the population with incomes less than or equal to y is given by $F(y) = 1 - [\underline{y}/y]^{\alpha}$. Now consider another quantity w related to y by the formula $w = Ay^{b}$, where of course the minimum value of w is $\underline{w} = A\underline{y}^{b}$. Then we see that $\underline{y}/y = [\underline{w}/w]^{1/b}$. Substituting in the formula for F we find $F(w) = 1 - [\underline{w}/w]^{\alpha/b}$. In other words the transformed variable also has the Pareto distribution with parameters $\underline{w}$ and α/b. Therefore we once again have the simple result that if pre-tax incomes are distributed according to the Pareto law, and if the tax system is closely approximated by the constant residual progression formula, then post-tax incomes are also distributed according to the Pareto law.

HOW GOOD ARE THE FORMULAS?

An obviously important criterion of suitability of a functional form is that it should roughly approximate the facts we wish to examine. It is too much to hope that one formula is going to fit some of the data all of the time or all of the data some of the time, but if it fits a non-negligible amount of the data a non-negligible amount of the time then the mathematical convenience of the formula may count for a great deal. One immediate difficulty is that the suitability of the functional form will depend on the kind of data being analysed. I shall deal with this by arbitrarily discussing four subject areas which are of particular economic interest. In doing so I am giving a mere sketch of the facts which may provide those interested with a motivation to enquire further.

Aitchison and Brown (1957) argued that the lognormal

hypothesis was particularly appropriate for the *distribution of earnings* in fairly homogeneous sections of the workforce. Thus, for example, in British agriculture in 1950 we find that the distribution of earnings among cowmen, the distribution among horsemen, that among stockmen and that among market gardeners proves in each case to be close to the lognormal. This evidence is also borne out in other sectors of the labour market. Weiss (1972) shows the satisfactory nature of the hypothesis of lognormality for graduate scientists' earnings in different areas of employment – particularly for those who were receiving more than $10,000 a year.

When we look at more comprehensive populations a difficulty arises in that the aggregate of several distinct lognormal distributions may not itself be lognormal. Suppose you have a number of different subgroups within the population (for example cowmen, horsemen, stockmen, etc.) and within each subgroup the distribution in the resulting population (all agricultural workers) will only be lognormal if, among other things, the dispersion parameter σ^2 may be taken as uniform throughout the groups. If your lognormal pigmen have a higher σ^2 than your lognormal tractor drivers. then you are in trouble. Possibly because this restrictive condition is not generally satisfied, systematic departures from lognormality are evident in many earnings distributions. Hence Lydall (1968) in attempting to find a general description of his 'standard distribution' of pretax wages and salaries for all adult non-agricultural workers makes the following observations. The central part of the distribution (from about the 10th percentile to the 80th percentile) is approximately lognormal. But the observed distribution has more of its population in its tails than a member of the lognormal family should have. In fact the upper tail (about the top 20% of the population) approximates more closely to the Pareto distribution.

If we are going to use current receipts as some surrogate measure of economic welfare then it is clear that a more comprehensive definition of income is appropriate. When we examine the *distribution of income* (from all sources) we find that the lognormal assumption is less satisfactory, for reasons similar to those which we discussed when dealing with the aggregation of earnings – compare the logarithmic transformation in figure 2-4 with the 'ideal' shape of figure 4-1. We are quite likely to find substantial departures at the lower tail, for reasons that are discussed in the next chapter. However, for the middle part of the income distribution, lognormality remains a reasonable assumption in many instances, and the assumption of a Paretian upper tail remains remarkably satisfactory, as the evidence of figure 4-5 bears out. In the case of incomes, the values of α tend to be in the range 1.5 to 2.5 and generally reveal a secularly increasing trend – see table 4-1. As we have seen it is this close approximation of the upper tail which led to some of the more optimistic conjectures of Pareto's disciples. It is perhaps otiose to mention that since Pareto's data necessarily related to high incomes alone, his law can hardly be expected to apply to the income distribution as a whole.

The 'Paretian upper tail' that has emerged from a study of income distributions works well for the *distribution of wealth*. There is a superficial reason to suppose that a curve like Pareto's might be useful in this application.

100

Table 4-1

Pareto's α for income distribution in the UK and the USA

UK		USA	
1688	1.58	1866-71	1.40 - 1.48
1812	1.31	1914	1.54
1843	1.50	1919	1.71
1867	1.47	1924	1.67
1893	1.50	1929	1.42
1918	1.47	1934	1.78
1937-38	1.57	1938	1.77
1944-45	1.75	1941	1.87
		1945	1.95
1949-50	1.95		
1954-55	2.10		
1959-60	2.32		
1964-65	2.33		
1969-70	2.55		

Sources: For UK 1949 onwards, Board of Inland Revenue
(1972, p.2). Other data taken from Bronfenbrenner
(1971, p.46)
Note: Figures refer to income before tax

Wealth data are usually compiled with any accuracy only for
the moderately wealthy and above. Hence - excluding those
whose wealth is unrecorded - we typically find a single-
tailed distribution. Evidence on the linearity of the Pareto
diagram (and hence on the close fit of the Pareto formula)
is demonstrated admirably by the Swedish data examined by
Steindl (1965) where α is about 1.5 to 1.7. Once again, we
usually find an increase in α over time indicating, for that
part of the distribution where the Paretian approximation is
suitable, a trend toward greater equality.

For our final application, the analysis of the
distribution of firms by size, succinct presentation of the
evidence and comparison with the special functional forms
can be found in Hart and Prais (for the UK) and in Steindl
(for the USA and Germany). The Pareto law only works for a

small number of firms that happen to be very large - but, as Steindl points out, although this represents a small proportion of individual business units, it accounts for a large proportion of total corporate assets. You typically find α in the (rather low) 1.0 to 1.5 range. However, the lognormal functional form fits a large number of distributions of firms by size - where size can variously be taken to mean corporate assets, turnover or number of employees. These approximations work best when industries are taken in broad groupings rather than individually.

This preliminary glimpse of evidence is perhaps sufficient to reinforce three conclusions which may have suggested themselves earlier in the discussion.

1. Neither the Pareto nor the lognormal hypothesis provides a 'law' of distribution in the strict sense that one particular member of either family is an exact model of income or wealth distribution in the long run. In particular it is nonsense to suppose that the Pareto curve (where applicable) should remain stable over long periods of history. As it happens, α is increasing nearly everywhere.

2. However, interpreting the Pareto or the lognormal 'law' as a description of the *shape* of particular distributions is more promising. Neither hypothesis usually works *very* well,[†] since the real world is too complicated for this, unless we look at a very narrow and well-defined piece of the real world such as the earnings of cowmen or the wealth of people with more than 100,000 kronor.

3. Nevertheless one or other functional form is a reasonable approximation in a heartening number of cases. The short cuts in empirical analysis that are thus made

---

† See the next chapter for a brief mention of the criteria of fit.

possible amply repay the trouble of understanding the mechanics of the mathematical formulas in the first place.

This simplification will perhaps be more readily understood when we come to wrestle with some of the difficulties that arise in the next chapter.

5
From theory to practice

'What would life be without arithmetic, but
a scene of horrors?'

　　　　　　　　　　　　　　- Rev. Sydney Smith (1835)

So where do we go now? One perfectly reasonable answer to
this would be to return to some of the knotty theoretical
issues to which we accorded only scant attention earlier.

Were we to follow this course, however, we should neg-
lect a large number of issues which must be wrestled with
before our ideas on inequality can be applied to numbers
culled from the real world. In this chapter we shall review
these problems in a fairly general way, since many of them
arise in the same form whatever concept of income, wealth
or other personal attribute is examined, and whatever the
national or international source from which the data are
drawn.

It is expedient to subdivide the practical problems
that we shall meet into five groups: (i) those associated
with the original data; (ii) those arising from computations
using the data; (iii) those involved in an appraisal of
the significance of these calculations; (iv) those

connected with special functional forms; (v) the interpretation of results.

THE DATA

The primary problem to be dealt with by anyone doing
quantitative research into inequality is that of defining
the variable y which we have loosely called 'income', and
then getting observations on it. In this section we deal
with some of these conceptual and practical issues.

For certain specific problem areas the choice of
variable and of source material is immediately apparent.
For example, if one is interested in the inequality of
voting power in a political system, the relevant variable
is the number of seats allocated per thousand of the
population (i.e. the fraction of a representative held by a
voting individual); in this situation it is a straightforward step to impute an index of voting power to each
member of the electorate. However, in a great many situations where inequality measures are applied, a number of
detailed preliminary considerations about the nature of the
'income' variable, y, and the way it is observed in practice
are in order. The reasons for this lie not only in the technique of measurement itself but also in the economic welfare connotations attached to the variable y. For in such
cases we typically find that a study of the distribution
of income or wealth is being used as a surrogate for the
distribution of an index of individual well-being. We shall
consider further some of the problems of interpreting the
data in this way once we have looked at the manner in which
the figures are obtained.

There are basically two ways of collecting this kind of
information: 1 You can ask people for it. 2 You can make

106

them give it to you. Neither method is wholly satisfactory since, in the first case, some people may choose not to give the information, or may give it incorrectly, and in the second case, the legal requirement for information may not correspond exactly to the data requirements of the social analyst. Let us look more closely at what is involved.

Method 1 This approach is commonly used by those organisations that desire the raw information for its own sake. It involves the construction of a carefully stratified (and thus representative) sample of the population, and then requesting the members of this sample to give the information that is required about their income, wealth, types of assetholding, spending patterns, household composition, etc. This method is used in the UK's *Family Expenditure Survey*, and in the *Current Population Surveys* conducted by the US Bureau of the Census. Obviously the principal difficulty is, as I mentioned, that of non-response or misinformation by those approached in the survey. The presumption is that disproportionately many of those refusing to cooperate will be among the rich, and thus a potentially significant bias may be introduced into the results. However, the response rate in some of the major surveys is surprisingly good (typically some 60% to 80%), and usually the raw data are weighted in order to mitigate the effect of non-response bias. A manifest advantage of this method of data collection is that if a person volunteers to take part in a survey, it may be possible to secure much more detailed and diverse information than could be arranged under a method involving compulsion, thus potentially broadening the scope of social enquiry.

Method 2 Useful information on income and wealth is often obtained as a by-product to such tiresome official obligations as making tax returns. The advantages of this conscript data over the volunteered survey data are obvious. Except where the tax administration is extremely informal (as is commonly supposed to be true in some Mediterranean countries) such that evasion introduces a substantial bias, it is generally possible to obtain a larger and more representative sample of the population. Nonresponse bias is less important, and it may be that in some countries legal penalties act as a suitable guarantee to ensure the minimum of misinformation. However, the drawbacks of such data are equally evident. In the study of income distributions, the income concept is that for which it is expedient for the authorities to define the tax base, rather than a person's 'net accretion of economic power between two points in time',[†] which is considered to be ideal for the purposes of the economist. Hence many components of a comprehensive definition of income - such as capital gains, fringe benefits, home production, the imputed value of leisure time and of owner-occupancy - may be imperfectly recorded, if recorded at all. Indeed, one may suppose that frequently both the rich and the not-so-rich will have taken steps legally to avoid the tax by transforming some part of their income into non-taxable (and unpublished) forms.[¶] Furthermore the sample population whose income or wealth is reported in the official figures often inaccurately represents the poor, since those with income or wealth below the tax exemption limit may either be excluded, or be recorded in insufficient detail.

---

† Royal Commission on the Taxation of Profits and Income (1955), p. 355.

¶ These warnings apply with increased emphasis in the case of wealth.

With little mental effort, then, we see that the practical definition of the variable y is only going to be as good as the way in which the information on it is compiled. So if you, as a student of inequality, are being asked to 'buy' a particular set of data on income or wealth, what should you watch out for? For a quick assessment, try the following checklist:

THE VARIABLE y:

A USER's GUIDE

1 What is included?

2 Which heads are counted, and who shares in the cake?

3 To what time period does it relate?

4 What valuation procedure has been used?

5 Which economic assumptions have been made?

Let us briefly examine each of these.

1. Recalling the argument of Chapter 1, if we concern ourselves with a narrowly defined problem, there is relatively little difficulty: an inquiry into, say, the inequality in earnings in some particular occupation will probably require a simple definition of the income variable. I shall use this approach later in the chapter when we look at inequality in the income reported to the tax authorities in the USA. For a wide interpretation of inequality, of course, you obviously need to reflect on whether the definition of income is as all-embracing as suggested on page 108 that it should be. Furthermore, if you want to arrive at people's *disposable* incomes, then careful consideration must be given to the adjustment that has been made for direct and indirect taxes, for social security

benefits and other money transfer incomes, and for benefits
received 'in kind' from the state, such as education.

2. The answer to 'whose heads should be counted?' is
obvious in some cases - for example in a study of the distribution of voting power one considers each enfranchised
person. In other cases, such as those where tax returns are
used, the choice of 'heads' is made for us - they are the
'tax units', which (for income data) sometimes means all men
and women individually, but more usually refers to nuclear
families and to unrelated individuals. For wealth data, the
unit is in general a single 'estate', the benefits of which
may be enjoyed by one person, or by a number in a family
group. Unfortunately detailed information such as family
composition of the income or wealth-holding tax-units is
available for few countries, whereas this detail *can* usually
be obtained from voluntary sample surveys. Under these circumstances one may allow for differing family size by
looking at income *per capita*, or at income per 'equivalent
adult', where it is desired to make a more precise adjustment for differential need. In doing this, of course, one
needs to include the incomes of all the people in one unit:
husband and wife, dependent children and so on. The latter
procedure involves counting each child as 'half an adult',
say, and then working out the distribution for the
fictitious 'adult-equivalent heads', which usually results
in a lower level of measured inequality than if the family
itself is taken as the basic population unit in the analysis.
You may well conclude that big enough problems are raised
in dealing with the heterogeneous people who are there in
the sampled population; but an even bigger problem is posed
by those who aren't there. This remark applies generally to
tax-based data, and particularly to wealth. Only those

estates that are sufficiently extensive to attract the attention of the tax man are usually included in the data, and hence there is a large proportion of the population which although not destitute does not appear in the published figures. So you must *either* (a) leave these people out altogether, and underestimate the amount of inequality; *or* (b) include them, but with zero wealth, and thus over-estimate inequality; *or* (c) by using information from alternative sources on *total* wealth, make some estimate of the wealth to be imputed *per capita* or (more ambitiously) guess at the distribution among these excluded persons.

3. Income (as opposed to wealth) is defined relative to a particular time unit, and you will generally find that measured inequality is noticeably lower if the personal income concept relates to a relatively long period than if quite a short time interval such as a week or a month is considered. The reason is simply that people's incomes fluctuate, and the longer you make the time unit, the more you 'average out' this volatility. As we noted in Chapter 1 the ultimate extension of this is to examine the distribution of lifetime average income. However, apart from the conceptual difficulties involved, sufficiently detailed data are just not available, and fairly sophisticated computer techniques must be used to draw inferences about the interpersonal distribution of this quantity.

4. In addition to the problem of incorporating non-monetary items[†] into the income or wealth aggregate, the question of the valuation procedure arises particularly when analysing trends of inequality over time, or in making comparisons between countries. For, when looking at time

---

† Such as income in kind or, in the case of wealth, assets for which no easily recognised market price exists.

trends we must recognise that changes in consumer goods'
prices will affect the purchasing power of the poor and of
the rich in different ways if the spending patterns of these
two groups are significantly different. The indications are
that in some advanced economies during the recent past,
price increases happen to have affected necessities disproportionately more than luxuries, and as a consequence
looking at inequality purely in money-income terms conceals
an increasing trend in inequality of real purchasing power.
If one wants to compare inequality within different
countries, or to examine inequality *among* countries in *per
capita* income, then even worse trouble lies ahead. One
must wrestle with diverse definitions of income, differing
relative prices (as in the time trend problem), different
levels and forms of public expenditure, and artificial
exchange rates – which collectively are giants barring the
way to comparability in income- or wealth-valuation.

5. To procure certain versions of the income or wealth
variable some economic sleight-of-hand is essential, and
it is important to grasp the legitimate tricks involved. I
shall mention two of these. (a) How does one allow for
people's reactions to price and income changes? Taxation
generally involves distortion of prices – those of commodities, and the value of time available for work. Now
people's choices of the amount they work and the amount they
save may be affected by changes in these prices, which means
in turn that the income distribution itself is affected. So
if you want to infer from the published figures what the
shape of the income distribution *would* be without government intervention, you must allow for this income response,
which in practice usually means flatly ignoring it. This
remark applies to the effects of indirect taxation as well

as to income tax. (b) What markets are assumed to exist?
Time and again one has to sum unlike components in an income
or wealth aggregate. To get an overall measure of net worth
one adds a man's current wealth (in terms of marketable
assets) to a present valuation of future income receipts
from other sources. To evaluate a family's disposable
income after all forms of intervention one must include the
value of non-monetary government transfers along with money
income. Either exercise involves not only the selection of
prices (mentioned in 4.) but usually a tacit assumption
about the existence of efficiently-operating markets for
capital and for government-provided goods. To see this, note
that a man with high future income but low current wealth
can only be said to be as well off as a man with high current
wealth but low income prospects if it is possible to borrow
from the capital market on the strength of one's anticipated
high earnings.

Taking your cue from the Rev. S. Smith, you might think
that enough 'horrors' had been met in just examining the
data. But we must press on.

COMPUTATION OF THE INEQUALITY MEASURES

This section assumes that you have decided on the
variable y that you wish to use, and the source from which
you are going to extract the data. As we shall see, there
are some potentially significant problems associated with
the arithmetic involved in proceeding from a table of raw
data to a number giving the realised value of an inequality
measure. We proceed by describing a number of inequality
measures that were introduced in Chapters 2 and 3 in a
formal but economical manner, and then using this presentation to explore the practical difficulties.

Suppose that for a particular population you know the
theoretical density function $f(y)$, which gives the proportion of the population that has an income in the infini-
tesimal interval y to $y + dy$.[†] This function is defined so
that if it is summed over the entire income range the result
is exactly one; formally:

$$\int_0^\infty f(y)\ dy = 1.$$

Now let us suppose that the desired inequality measure, or
an ordinally equivalent transformation of the desired
inequality measure, can be written in the form

$$J = \int_0^\infty h(y) \cdot f(y)\ dy \tag{1}$$

where $h(.)$ is some function of y that we have yet to specify.
It so happens that nearly every inequality measure that is
of interest, except the Gini coefficient, can be shown to
be ordinally equivalent to a form such as (1) - mathematically inclined readers are invited to check this from the
table in the appendix. Some can be written exactly in this
fashion - for example the relative mean deviation for which
we would take $h(y)$ to be $|y/\bar{y} - 1|$, or Theil's inequality

---

† For those who are uneasy about integration an intuitive
  description may help. Suppose that you have a diagram of
  a smooth curve $\phi(y)$, drawn with y measured 'horizontally'
  and ϕ 'vertically'. Then $\int_a^b \phi(y)\ dy$ means the area under
  the curve, above the horizontal axis and bounded on either
  side by the vertical lines $y = a$ and $y = b$. Thus, in
  figure 2-2a, $\int_{3000}^{4000} f(y)\ dy$ means the area between the
  smooth curve and the line OF that also lies between the
  points C and D. Instead of working out one single rect-
  angle $CDD'C'$, it is as though we calculated the area of
  lots of rectangles of tiny base width made to fit under
  the curve along CD. Hence the '$\int$' sign can be taken as
  something quite similar to the summation sign 'Σ'.

114

measure for which we define $h(y)$ to be $[y/\bar{y}]\ \log(y/\bar{y})$.
Others are related to (1) by a simple transformation – for
example if we take $h(y)$ to be $[y/\bar{y}]^{1-\varepsilon}$ and then consider
the transformation $1 - J^{1/1-\varepsilon}$ we find that we have A_ε,
Atkinson's inequality measure with inequality aversion para-
meter ε. It is worth re-emphasising that, as long as we
have defined a sensible inequality measure, the exact form
of $h(y)$ does not matter at all, and formula (1) is just a
neat way of describing a large number of measures.

However, equation (1) gives the inequality measure in
its theoretical form using a continuous distribution function. One might specify such a continuous function (for
example, the lognormal or the Pareto form) as a rough and
ready approximation to the facts about the distribution of
income, wealth, etc.; the problems associated with this
procedure are taken up later. However, in practice we may
not wish to use such approximating devices, and we would
then want to know what modifications need to be made to
formula (1) in order to use it directly with actual data.

First of all, let us note that if we are presented with
n actual observations y_1, y_2, y_3, ..., y_n of all n people's
incomes, some of our problems are virtually over. It is
appropriate simply to replace formula (1) with its discrete
equivalent:

$$J = \frac{1}{n} \sum_{i=1}^{n} h(y_i). \qquad (2)$$

What this means is that we work out the $h(y)$ function for
Mr Jones and add it to the value of the function for
Ms Smith, and add it to that of Mr Singh, and so on.

It is a fairly simple step to proceed to the construction of a Lorenz curve and to calculate the associated

Gini coefficient. There are several ways of carrying out
the routine computations, but the following is straightforward enough. Arrange all the incomes into 'Parade'
order, so that y_1 is the largest income, y_2 the next
largest, and so on down to man n. For the Lorenz curve,
mark off the horizontal scale (the line OC in figure 2-3)
into n equal intervals. Plot the first point on the curve
just above the endpoint of the first interval at a 'height'
of $y_n/n\bar{y}$; plot the second at the end of the second interval
at a height of $[y_{n-1} + y_n]/n\bar{y}$; the third at the end of the
third interval at a height $[y_{n-2} + y_{n-1} + y_n]/n\bar{y}$; ... and
so on. You can calculate the Gini coefficient from the
following easy formula:

$$G = 1 + \frac{1}{n} - \frac{2}{n^2\bar{y}}\left[y_1 + 2y_2 + 3y_3 + \ldots + ny_n\right].$$

Unfortunately, in many interesting fields of study,
these procedures are not entirely suitable for the lay
investigator into inequality for two reasons. Firstly, most
of the published and accessible data on incomes, wealth,
etc. is presented in *grouped* form, rather than as individual
records. Secondly, many of the important sets of ungrouped
data that are available are not easily manipulated by the
layman, unless he is a layman with a 2-megabyte computer
to hand. The problem derives not from mathematical intrac-
tability – the computational techniques would be much as I
have just described – but from the vast quantity of information typically involved. An 'important' study with ungrouped data usually involves the coverage of a large and
heterogeneous population, which means that n may be a number
of the order of tens of thousands. Such sets of data are
normally obtained from computerised records of tax returns,

survey interviews and the like, and the basic problems of
handling and preparing the information require large-scale
data-processing techniques.

If we have less ambitious practical uses in mind, we
must obviously turn to a consideration of grouped distributions. Were we to examine a typical source of information
on income or wealth distributions, we should probably find
that the facts are presented in the following way. 'In the
year in question, n_1 people had at least $\$a_1$ and less than
$\$a_2$; n_2 people had at least $\$a_2$ and less than $\$a_3$; n_3
people had at least $\$a_3$ and less than $\$a_4$, ...'. In
addition we may be told that the average income of people
in the first group ($\$a_1$ to $\$a_2$) was reported to be $\$\mu_1$,
average income in the second group ($\$a_2$ to $\$a_3$) turned out
to be $\$\mu_2$, and so on. Columns 1-4 of table 5-1 are an
example of this kind of presentation. Notice the difference
between having the luxury of knowing the *individual* incomes
y_1, y_2, y_3, ..., y_n and of having to make do with knowing
the numbers of people falling between the *arbitrary class
limits* a_1, a_2, a_3, ... which have been set by the compilers
of the official statistics.

Suppose that these compilers of statistics have chopped
up the income range into a total of k intervals:

$$(a_1, a_2) \quad (a_2, a_3) \quad (a_3, a_4) \cdots (a_k, a_{k+1}).$$

If we assume for the moment that $a_1 = 0$ and $a_{k+1} = \infty$, then
we have indeed neatly subdivided our entire theoretical
range, zero to infinity; (these assumptions will not do in
practice as we shall soon see). Accordingly, the theoretical
formula (1) may be modified to:

$$\int_{a_1}^{a_2} h(y)f(y)\,dy + \int_{a_2}^{a_3} h(y)f(y)\,dy + \ldots + \int_{a_k}^{a_{k+1}} h(y)f(y)\,dy,$$

Table 5-1

Individual Income Returns: USA 1972

Group no.	Income range	Number in groups	Group mean (dollars)	Relative pop.freq. (%)	Cumulative percentages Population	Incomes
(1)	(2)	(3)	(4)	(5)	(6)	(7)
(1)†	No positive income	440,435	-7,198†	---	---	---
(2)	$1 - $999	5,671,422	545	7.35	7.35	0.41
(3)	$1,000 - $1,999	5,860,523	1,496	7.60	14.95	1.58
(4)	$2,000 - $2,999	4,980,988	2,489	6.46	21.41	3.24
(5)	$3,000 - $3,999	4,954,358	3,501	6.42	27.83	5.55
(6)	$4,000 - $4,999	5,055,586	4,487	6.55	34.39	8.58
(7)	$5,000 - $5,999	4,731,472	5,495	6.13	40.52	12.05
(8)	$6,000 - $6,999	4,251,533	6,502	5.51	46.03	15.74
(9)	$7,000 - $7,999	4,272,799	7,492	5.54	51.57	20.02
(10)	$8,000 - $8,999	4,020,655	8,492	5.21	56.78	24.58
(11)	$9,000 - $9,999	3,899,385	9,488	5.06	61.84	29.52
(12)	$10,000 - $10,999	3,641,679	10,495	4.72	66.56	34.62
(13)	$11,000 - $11,999	3,460,349	11,494	4.49	71.05	39.93
(14)	$12,000 - $12,999	3,107,882	12,493	4.03	75.08	45.12
(15)	$13,000 - $13,999	2,781,429	13,476	3.61	78.68	50.12
(16)	$14,000 - $14,999	2,372,816	14,480	3.08	81.76	54.71
(17)	$15,000 - $19,999	7,773,413	17,142	10.08	91.84	72.50
(18)	$20,000 - $24,999	3,093,728	22,123	4.01	95.85	81.64
(19)	$25,000 - $29,999	1,266,377	27,177	1.64	97.49	86.24

(20)	$30,000 - $49,999	1,337,578	37,066	1.73	99.22	92.86
(21)	$50,000 - $99,999	483,677	66,125	0.627	99.851	97.13
(22)	$100,000 - $199,999	91,707	130,776	0.119	99.970	98.73
(23)	$200,000 - $499,999	19,233	281,547	0.025	99.995	99.45
(24)	$500,000 - $999,999	2,666	671,890	0.004	99.999	99.69
(25)	$1,000,000 and over	1,030	2,234,352	0.001	100.000	100.00
	Total population$_\dagger$:	77,572,730		100.000		
	Pop. with positive inc.:	77,132,295				
	Total income† ($,000)$_\dagger$:	748,924,766				
	Population mean income†:	$9,710				

$\dagger$ Nonpositive incomes are excluded from calculation of frequencies, total income and mean income.

¶ Discrepancies in subtotals are due to rounding errors.
Source: Internal Revenue Service, *Statistics of Income: Individual Tax Returns.*

which can be written more simply:

$$J = \sum_{i=1}^{k} \int_{a_i}^{a_{i+1}} h(y)\, f(y)\ dy. \tag{3}$$

It may be worth repeating that this is exactly the same formula as equation (1), the only notational difference being that the income range has been subdivided into k 'pieces'. However, although we have observations on the average income and the number of people in each class (a_i, a_{i+1}), we probably have not the faintest idea what the distribution $f(y)$ looks like within each class. How can we get round this problem?

A simple first step is to calculate from the available information upper and lower limits on the unknown theoretical value J. That is, we compute two numbers J_L and J_U such that it is certain that

$$J_L \leq J \leq J_U , \tag{4}$$

even though the value of J is unknown.

The lower limit J_L is found by assuming that everyone in the first class gets the average income in that class, $\$\mu_1$, and everyone in the second class gets the average income in that class, $\$\mu_2$, and so on; i.e. to compute J_L one imagines that there is *no* inequality *within* classes. Suppose that there are n_i people in the ith class (a_i, a_{i+1}) and n people in the whole population – column 5 in table 5-1 records the resultant *relative frequencies* n_i/n for each income class. Using these relative frequencies we then have:

$$J_L = \sum_{i=1}^{k} \frac{n_i}{n} h(\mu_i) \tag{5}$$

120

Notice that if we are given the average income in each class, μ_1, μ_2, μ_3, $\ldots$, μ_k, we do not need to know the class limits a_1, a_2, a_3, $\ldots$, a_k, a_{k+1} in order to calculate J_L. In contrast, the upper limit J_U is found by assuming that there is *maximum* inequality *within* each class, subject to the condition that the assumed average income within the class tallies with the observed number μ_i. So we assume that in class 1 everyone gets *either* \$$a_1$ *or* \$$a_2$, but that no one actually receives any intermediate income. If we let a proportion $\lambda_1 = [a_2 - \mu_1]/[a_2 - a_1]$ of the class 1 occupants be stuck at the lower limit, \$$a_1$, and a proportion on $1 - \lambda_1$ of class 1 occupants receive the upper limit income \$$a_2$, then one obtains the right answer for average income within the class, namely \$$\mu_1$. Repeating this procedure for the other income classes and using the general definition $\lambda_i = [a_{i+1} - \mu_i]/[a_{i+1} - a_i]$ we may now write:

$$J_U = \sum_{i=1}^{k} \frac{n_i}{n} \left[\lambda_i h(a_i) + [1-\lambda_i] h(a_{i+1}) \right] \tag{6}$$

A similar procedure can be carried out for the Gini index. We have:

$$G_L = \tfrac{1}{2} \sum_{i=1}^{k} \sum_{j=1}^{k} \frac{n_i n_j}{n^2 \bar{y}} |\mu_i - \mu_j| ,$$

$$G_U = G_L + \sum_{i=1}^{k} \frac{n_i^2}{n^2 \bar{y}} \lambda_i [\mu_i - a_i].$$

We now have our two numbers J_L, J_U which satisfy the property given in relation (4). The strengths of this procedure are that we have not had to make *any* assumption about the underlying theoretical distribution $f(y)$ and that the calculations required in working out formulas (5)

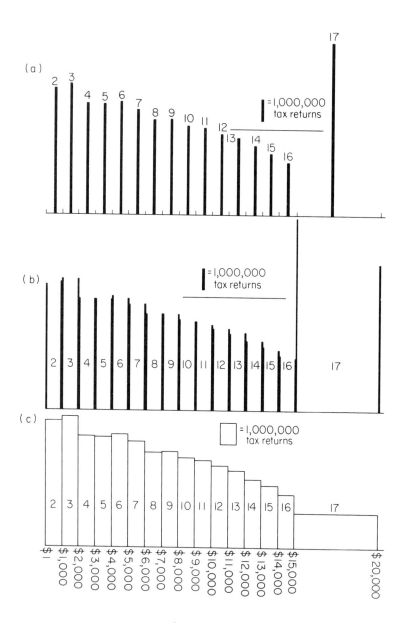

Figure 5-1

and (6) in practice are simple enough to be carried out on an unsophisticated pocket calculator. The procedure by which the two numbers are derived is illustrated in figure 5-1: part (a) shows the population assembled at the group means of the first 17 income classes of the data in table 5-1; part (b) has the population clustered at the interval boundaries in the proportions described above; part (c) is simply for reference - it shows for the same data the conventional histogram introduced in figure 2-2a in which the population within each class is assumed uniformly distributed over the class.

To demonstrate the practical significance of the divergence between J_L and J_U, columns 1 to 4 of table 5-2 have been constructed from the data of table 5-1, on the assumption that the lowest possible income, a_1, was \$1 and that the highest possible income, a_{k+1}, was \$4,000,000. It is obvious from the values of the five inequality measures recorded that the size of the gap $J_U - J_L$ as a proportion of J's compromise value varies a great deal from one measure to another. While this gap is a mere fraction of one percent for the relative mean deviation or the Gini coefficient, it is appreciably large for the coefficient of variation[†] and the logarithmic variance. These results may be sensitive to the assumptions made about the two extreme incomes a_1 (\$1) and a_{k+1} (\$4,000,000). To investigate this, let us first look at the calculations after all income-receivers below \$1,000 have been eliminated (metaphorically speaking) - see columns 5 to 8 of table 5-2. As we expect,

---

† We recall that c is not written exactly in the form of equation (1). However, the Herfindahl index, $H = [c^2 + 1]/n$ can be written this way. The gap between J_L and J_U for H is about 15%.

Table 5-2

	Income Class ($1, $999) Included				Income Class ($1, $999) Excluded			
	lower J_L (1)	upper J_U (2)	compromise (3)	% difference (4)	lower J_L (5)	upper J_U (6)	compromise (7)	% difference (8)
Rel. mean deviation	.6464	.6479	.6468	(0.2)	.5917	.5938	.5926	(0.4)
Coeff. of variation	1.4175	1.5742	1.4712	(10.7)	1.3457	1.4996	1.3985	(11.0)
log. variance	1.2905	3.7460	1.4526	(169.0)	.7767	.8196	.7907	(5.4)
Gini	.4537	.4566	.4556	(0.6)	.4165	.4195	.4185	(0.7)
Theil	.3917	.4059	.3962	(3.6)	.3330	.3449	.3369	(3.5)

Notes. 1. Source as for table 5-1.
2. Cols. (5)-(8) computed as for cols. (1)-(4) except that distribution is truncated below $1,000.
3. 'Compromise' is found by fitting a Pareto density function within each income class.
4. Col. (4) calculated as $((2)-(1)) \div (3) \times 100$. Col. (8) similarly derived.

for all the measures the amount of inequality is less for
the distribution now truncated at the lower end. But the
really significant point is that the enormous range of
possible values for the logarithmic variance revealed in
column 4 has now been drastically cut, although the revised
difference (in column 8) may still not be regarded as
negligible. This suggests that the practical usefulness of
this measure depends crucially on the way lower incomes are
treated in grouped distributions – a point to which we
return in the next section when considering SWF-based
measures. Now consider the upper tail. It is no good putting
$a_{k+1} = \infty$, because for many inequality measures this results
in J_U taking on the 'complete inequality' value, whatever
the rest of the distribution looks like (this problem can
also arise if you put $a_1 = 0$). If the average income in
each class is known, the simplest solution is to make a
sensible guess as I have done above. To see how important
this guess is, the figures were reworked for a number of
values of a_{k+1}. The only measure whose value changes significantly was the coefficient of variation, for which the
results are plotted in figure 5-2.

Let us now see how to draw a Lorenz curve. From column
5 of table 5-1 construct column 6 in an obvious way by calculating a series of running totals. Next calculate the percentage of total income accounted for in each interval by
multiplying each element of column 5 by the corresponding
number in column 4 and dividing by the population mean;
calculate the cumulative percentages as before by working
out running totals – this gives you column 7. Columns 6
(population shares) and 7 (income shares) form a set of
observed points on the Lorenz curve for the US Internal
Revenue Service data relating to 1972. Some of these

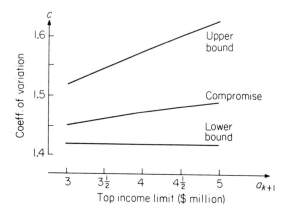

Source: Table 5-1

Figure 5-2

(a)

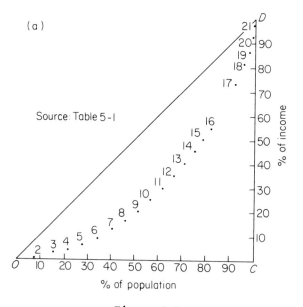

Source: Table 5-1

% of population

Figure 5-3a

126

points[†] are plotted in figure 5-3a. We now have a problem similar to those which occur so frequently in my son's playbooks – join up the dots.

However this is not as innocuous as it seems, because there are infinitely many curves that may be sketched in, subject to only three restrictions, mentioned below. Each such curve drawn has associated with it an implicit assumption about the way in which income is distributed within the income classes, and hence about the 'true' value of the inequality measure that we wish to use. If the dots are joined by straight lines, then we are assuming that there is no inequality within income classes – in other words, this corresponds to the use of J_L, the lower bound on the calculated inequality measure. This method is shown in detail by the solid lines in figure 5-3b which is an

(b)

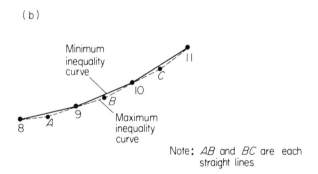

Note: *AB* and *BC* are each straight lines

Figure 5-3b

---

† Three of the upper observations have been left out of the diagram for reasons of clarity.

enlargement of the central portion of figure 5-3a. You can construct a maximum inequality Lorenz curve by drawing a line of slope $a_i/\bar{y}$ through the ith dot, repeating this for every dot, and then using the resulting broken line. This is illustrated by the dashed lines in figure 5-3b. Now we can state the three rules that any joining-up-the dot procedure must satisfy.

1. Any curve must go through all the dots, including the two vertices.

2. It must be convex to the point C. (These two rules ensure that the curve does not pass above the minimum-inequality Lorenz curve.)

3. It must not pass below the maximum inequality curve.

We may well want a 'compromise' curve satisfying these requirements because the observed points on the Lorenz curve in table 5-1 only give us the income shares of the bottom 7.35%, the bottom 14.95%, etc., whereas we would be more interested in the shares of, say, the bottom 10%, the bottom 20%, and to get these we must interpolate on a curve between the points. One suggestion is to use the Pareto interpolation formula (given in the appendix), which is much less fearsome than it looks, because you do not have to compute the parameters α, $\underline{y}$ along the way. All you need are the population and income shares. Unfortunately this simplicity is also its weakness. Because the formula does not use information about the a_is the resulting curve may violate condition 3. An alternative method which may be arranged so that all three conditions are satisfied is to fit a theoretical frequency distribution within each interval in figure 5-1, and work out the Lorenz curve from that. This is the procedure used for table 5-2 and figure 5-2, the details of which are in the appendix. Other methods of interpolation can be used to calculate the

128

compromise, but unfortunately it is not generally possible
to give a simple rule-of-thumb. One notable exception is
the Gini index; for this measure, the compromise can be
approximated by $\frac{2}{3} G_U + \frac{1}{3} G_L$ which works remarkably well for
most distributions, and may be verified from table 5-2.

APPRAISING THE CALCULATIONS

We have now seen how to calculate the indices themselves,
or bounds on these indices from the raw data. Taking these
calculations at face value, let us see how much significance
should be attached to the numbers that emerge.

The problem may be introduced by way of an example.
Suppose that you have comparable distribution data for two
years, 1970, 1975, and you want to know what has happened
to inequality between the two points in time. You compute
some inequality indices for each data set, let us say the
coefficient of variation, the relative mean deviation,
Theil's index, and the Gini index, so that two sets of
numbers result: $\{c_{1970}, \ M_{1970}, \ T_{1970}, \ G_{1970}\}$ and
$\{c_{1975}, \ M_{1975}, \ T_{1975}, \ G_{1975}\}$ each set giving a picture of
inequality in the appropriate year. You now have another
play-book puzzle - spot the difference between the two
pictures. This is, of course, a serious problem; we may
notice, say, that c_{1975} is 'a bit' lower than c_{1970} - but
is it noticeably lower, or are the two numbers 'about the
same'? Readers trained in statistical theory will have
detected in this a long and imprecise way round to introducing tests of significance.

However, given that we are looking at the difference
between the observed value of an inequality measure and
some base value (such as an earlier year's inequality)
there are three ways in which the word 'significance' can

be interpreted, as applied to this difference: (1) statistical significance in the light of variability due to the sampling procedure; (2) statistical significance in view of the arbitrary grouping of observations; (3) social/political significance. Item (3) properly belongs to the last section of this chapter. As far as items (1) and (2) are concerned, since space is not available for a proper discussion of statistical significance, I may perhaps be forgiven for mentioning only some rough guidelines - further reference may be made to the notes to this chapter.

Let us suppose that we are dealing with sampling variability in an *ungrouped* distribution (unfortunately, rigorous analysis with grouped data is difficult). The numbers y_1, y_2, y_3, ..., y_n are regarded as a sample of independent random observations. We perform the calculations described earlier and arrive at a number J. An essential piece of equipment for appraising this result is the *standard error*[†] of J which, given various assumptions about the underlying distribution of y and the manner of drawing the sample can be calculated from the observations y_1, ..., y_n. Since the y s are assumed to be random, the number J must also be taken to be an observation on a random variable. Given the theoretical distribution of the y s it is possible to derive in principle the distribution

---

[†] A couple of technical words of warning should be noted. Firstly, in an application we ought to examine carefully the character of the sample. If it is very large by comparison with the whole finite population, the formulas in the text must be modified; this is in fact the case in my worked example - although the qualitative conclusions remain valid. If it is non-random, the formulas may be misleading. Secondly for some of the exercises carried out we should really use standard error formulas for *differences* in the Js; but this is a complication which would not affect the character of our results.

of the values of the computed number J. The standard
deviation or square-root-of-variance of this derived distribution is known as the standard error of J. Given this
standard error an answer can be provided to the kind of
question raised earlier in this section: if the difference
$c_{1975} - c_{1970}$ is at least twice the standard error for c,
then it is 'quite likely' that the change in inequality
is not due to sampling variability alone; if this is at
least three times the standard error, then it is almost
certain that the change in c is not a result of sampling
variability and thus this drop *is* significant.

Some rule-of-thumb formulas for the standard errors
are readily obtainable if the sample size, n, is assumed to
be large.[†] For the coefficient of variation, c, the
standard error is $c\sqrt{[(1 + 2c^2)/n]}$; for the relative mean
deviation, M, it is $\sqrt{\{[M^2(c^2 - 1) + c^2]/n\}}$; the Gini coefficient's standard error is about $G\sqrt{[(c^2 + \frac{1}{2})/n]}$; and for
the variance of logarithms, v_1, the standard error is
$v_1\sqrt{(2/n)}$. I want to emphasise that these are *rough* approximations intended for those who want to get an intuitive
feel for the significance of numbers that may have been
worked out by hand.

I would like to encourage even those who do not like
formulas to notice from the above expressions that in each
case the standard error will become very small for a large
sample size n. Hence for a **sample as large** as that in
table 5-1, the sampling variability is likely to be quite

---

† For c and for G, the sampled distribution is assumed to
be normal; for M it is supposed to be symmetrical (including the normal, of course, as a special case); for v_1
it is assumed to be lognormal. Precise formulas can be
given that do not require these restrictions, but they
would be much more complex.

small in comparison with item (2), the range of possible values of the inequality measure on account of the grouping of the distribution. A quick illustration will perhaps suffice. Suppose for the moment that the compromise value of c = 1.4712 given in table 5-2 were the actual value computed from ungrouped data. What would the standard error be? Noting that the sample size is about 77 million, the standard error is about
1.471 × √{[1 + (2 × 1.471 × 1.471)] ÷ 77,000,000} ≈ 0.00039.
Hence we can be virtually certain that sampling variability introduces an error of no more than three times this, or ± 0.0012 on the ungrouped value of c. Contrast this with the gap $J_U - J_L$ = 0.1567 found from table 5-2. Hence for this kind of distribution, the grouping error may be of the order of one hundred times as large as the sampling variability.

As we have noted, the grouping variability may be large in comparison to the value of the measure itself. This poses an important question. Can the grouping variability be so large as to make certain inequality measures useless? The answer appears to be a qualified 'yes' in some cases. To see this, consider Atkinson's measure A_ε for the data of table 5-1. Instead of tabulating the calculations of the lower and upper bounds and compromise value as in table 5-2, let us represent them pictorially as in figure 5-4. Part (a) shows the problem that arises when lower incomes are included. For values of $\varepsilon \geqslant 1$, the range of possible values of the measure is extremely large. In fact for ε = 2, the range of possible values amounts to some 42% of the compromise value of the inequality measure itself. Obviously, then, it will be hard to say unequivocally whether A_2 is greater or less than it was in some other year simply

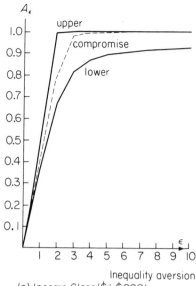

(a) Income Class ($1,$999)
Included

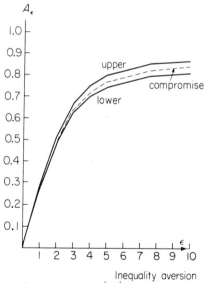

(b) Income Class ($1,$999)
Excluded

Figure 5-4

133

because the grouping bounds are so wide.

From part (b) of figure 5-4 it seems that we can greatly reduce the problem by cutting out the first income class as was done in table 5-2, although even after this drastic step the range of values is still large when $\varepsilon \geqslant 1$ (around 6-7% of the compromise A_ε). To do this (or to manipulate in some other way the assumption about a_1 which is causing all the trouble) is to avoid the problem, since we are deliberately ignoring incomes in the range where our inequality measure is designed to be particularly sensitive. The unpalatable conclusion is that because of grouping error (and perhaps sampling error too) *either* we shall have to discard certain sensitive measures of inequality from our toolkit on empirical grounds, *or* the distribution must provide extremely detailed information about low incomes so that measures with high inequality aversion can be used, *or* the income distribution figures will have to be truncated or doctored at the lower end in a way which may reduce their relevance in the particular area of social enquiry.

SHORTCUTS: FITTING FUNCTIONAL FORMS.[†]

And now for something completely different. Instead of attempting to work out inequality statistics from empirical distribution data directly, it may be expedient to fit a functional form to the raw data, and thus compute the inequality statistics by indirect means. The two steps involved are as follows. (1) Given the family of distributions represented by a certain functional form, estimate the parameter values which characterise the particular

---

† This section contains material of a more technical nature which the lay reader may omit without loss of continuity.

family member appropriate to the data. (2) Given the formula for a particular inequality measure in terms of the family parameters,[†] calculate the inequality statistics from the parameter estimates obtained in step (1). For the Pareto distribution, step (1) involves estimation of the parameter α from the data, and step (2) might be to write down the value of the Gini coefficient, which for the Pareto is simply $G = 1/[\,2\alpha - 1]$. For the lognormal distribution, the first step involves estimation of σ^2. Since the second step is simple once you have the formula (it usually involves merely an ordinally equivalent transformation of one of the parameters), I shall only consider further methods relating to step (1) in detail.

Two words of warning – up to now we have used symbols such as $\bar{y}$, V, etc. to denote the theoretical mean variance, etc., of some distribution. From now on, these symbols will represent the computed mean, variance, etc., of the set of observations that we have under consideration. Although this is a little sloppy, it avoids introducing more symbols. Also, note that often there is more than one satisfactory method of estimating a parameter value, yielding different results. Under such circumstances it is up to the user to decide on the relative merits of the alternative methods. Let us move straightaway on to the estimation of the parameters of the lognormal distribution for ungrouped and for grouped data.

If the data are in ungrouped form – that is we have n observations, y_1, y_2, $\ldots, y_n$ – then on the assumption that these come from a population that is lognormal, it is easy to use the so-called *method of moments* to calculate

---

† See the appendix for these formulas.

estimates $\tilde{\mu}$, $\tilde{\sigma}^2$ for the lognormal distribution. Calculate the mean, and the Herfindahl index for these n incomes (the sum of the squares of the shares – see p. 61:

$$H = \sum_{i=1}^{n} \left[y_i / n\bar{y} \right]^2 \ .$$

Then we find:

$$\tilde{\sigma}^2 = \log(nH) \tag{7}$$
$$\tilde{\mu} = \log \bar{y} - \tfrac{1}{2}\tilde{\sigma}^2 .$$

While this is very easy, it is not as efficient[†] as the following method.

An alternative procedure that is fairly easy for ungrouped data is to derive the *maximum likelihood estimates*, $\hat{\mu}, \hat{\sigma}^2$. To do this, transform all the observations $y_1, y_2, \ldots, y_n$ to their logarithms $x_1, x_2, \ldots, x_n$. Then calculate:

$$\hat{\mu} = \frac{1}{n} \sum_{i=1}^{n} x_i \tag{8}$$
$$\hat{\sigma}^2 = \frac{1}{n} \sum_{i=1}^{n} \left[x_i - \hat{\mu} \right]^2 .$$

It is evident that $\hat{\mu}$ is simply $\log y^*$ – the logarithm of the geometric mean, and that $\hat{\sigma}^2$ is v_1, the variance of the logarithms defined relative to y^*.

In the case of grouped data, maximum likelihood methods are available, but they are too involved to set out here. However, the method of moments can be applied similarly to the ungrouped case, provided that in the computation of H an appropriate correction is made to allow for the

---

[†] i.e. standard errors of the estimates will be larger than for the maximum likelihood procedure (which is the most efficient method in this case).

grouping of observation.

We shall go straight on now to consider the estimation of the parameters of the Pareto distribution, once again dealing first with ungrouped data. For the *method of moments*, pick from the n observations y_1, y_2, ..., y_n the lowest income and call it y_0. It can be shown that the *expected* value of this lowest observation (given the assumption that the sample has been drawn at random from a Pareto distribution with parameters α, $\underline{y}$), is $\alpha n \underline{y}/[\alpha n - 1]$. Work out the observed mean income $\bar{y}$. The *expected* value of this (given the same assumption) is $\alpha \underline{y}/[\alpha - 1]$ – see page 97. We now simply equate the sample observations (y_0 and $\bar{y}$) to their expected values:

$$y_0 = \alpha n \underline{y}/[\alpha n - 1]$$
$$\bar{y} = \alpha \underline{y}/[\alpha - 1]$$

Solving these two simple equations in two unknowns α, $\underline{y}$ we find the method-of-moments estimates for the two parameters:

$$\tilde{\alpha} = [\bar{y} - y_0/n] /[\bar{y} - y_0] \qquad (9)$$
$$\tilde{\underline{y}} = [1 - 1/\tilde{\alpha}]\bar{y}$$

However, this procedure is not suitable for grouped data. By contrast, the *ordinary least squares* method for estimating α can be applied whether the data are grouped or not. Recall that if y is any income level, and P is the proportion of the population with that income or more, then under the Pareto distribution, a linear relationship exists between $\log P$ and $\log y$ (see p. 91), the slope of the line being α. In fact we may write this as

$$p = z - \alpha x,$$

where p represents $\log P$, x represents $\log y$, and z gives the intercept of the straight line ($z = \alpha \log \underline{y}$).

Given a set of ungrouped observations y_1, y_2, ..., y_n arranged say in ascending size order, it is easy to set up the estimating equation for α. For the first observation, since the entire sample has that income or more ($P = 1$), the relevant value of p is $p_1 = \log 1 = 0$. For the second observation, we have $p_2 = \log(1 - 1/n)$; similarly for the third, $p_3 = \log(1 - 2/n)$, and for the fourth, $p_4 = \log(1 - 3/n)$, ... , and for the very last we have $p_n = \log(1 - [n - 1]/n) = \log(1/n)$. Given the values $x_1, x_2, x_3, ..., x_n$, (calculated from the y-values) we may then write down the following set of equations:

$$p_1 = z - \alpha x_1 + e_1$$
$$p_2 = z - \alpha x_2 + e_2$$
$$\cdots \qquad \cdots \qquad \cdots \tag{10}$$
$$p_n = z - \alpha x_n + e_n,$$

where $e_1, e_2, ..., e_n$ are error terms. One then proceeds to obtain least squares estimates of α and z in the usual way by minimising the sum of the squares of the es. In the case of grouped data, let f_i be the observed proportion of the population lying in the ith income interval, and take x_i to be $\log a_i$, that is the logarithm of the lower bound of the interval, for every interval $i = 1, 2, 3, ..., k$. The appropriate p_is are found by cumulating the f_is upwards from interval i and taking logarithms, thus:

$$p_1 = \log(1) = 0,$$
$$p_2 = \log(f_2 + f_3 + f_4 + \cdots + f_{k-1} + f_k),$$
$$p_3 = \log(\quad\; f_3 + f_4 + \cdots + f_{k-1} + f_k), \tag{11}$$
$$\cdots \quad \cdots \quad \cdots \quad \cdots \quad \cdots \quad \cdots$$
$$p_{k-1} = \log(\qquad\qquad\qquad\qquad f_{k-1} + f_k),$$
$$p_k = \log(\qquad\qquad\qquad\qquad\qquad f_k).$$

One then proceeds as before.

Of course you are at liberty to fit a lognormal, Pareto or some other function to any set of data you like, but this is only a useful occupation if a 'reasonable' fit is

138

obtained. What constitutes a 'reasonable' fit?

An answer that immediately comes to mind if you have used a regression technique is to use the correlation coefficient R^2. However, taking a high value of R^2 as a criterion of a satisfactory fit can be misleading when fitting a curve to a highly skewed distribution, since a close fit in the tail may mask substantial departures elsewhere. This caution applies also to line-of-eye judgements of suitability, especially where a log-transformation has been used, as in the construction of figure 4-5. For small samples, standard 'goodness-of-fit' tests such as the χ^2- criterion may be used, although for a large sample size n you may find that such tests *reject* the suitability of your fitted distribution even though on other grounds it may be a perfectly reasonable approximation.

An easy alternative method of discovering whether a particular formula is 'satisfactory' can be found using an inequality measure. Let us look at how it is done with grouped data and the Gini coefficient – the argument is easily extended. Work out G_L and G_U, the lower and upper limits on the 'true' value of the Gini. Given the fitted functional form, the Pareto let us say, we can calculate G_Π, the value of the Gini index on the supposition that the data actually follow the Pareto law. If $G_L \leqslant G_\Pi \leqslant G_U$ then it is reasonable to accept the Pareto functional form as a close approximation. What we are saying is that according to the concept of 'distance between incomes' implied by this inequality measure, it is impossible to distinguish the theoretical curve from the 'true' distribution underlying the observations. Of course, a different concept of distance may well produce a contradictory answer, but we have the advantage of specifying in advance the inequality measure that we find appropriate, and then testing accordingly. In my opinion this method does not provide a definitive test; but if the upper-and-lower-limit criterion is persistently violated for a number of inequality measures, there seems to be good reason for doubting the closeness of fit of the proposed functional form.

Let us apply this to the IRS data of table 5-1 and examine the Pareto law. Since we expect only higher incomes to follow this Law, we shall truncate incomes below $7,000. First of all we work out from column 5 or 6 of table 5-1 the numbers p_i as shown in equations (11), and the logarithms of the lower bounds a_i given in column 1 of table 5-1, in order to set up the regression equations (10). Using ordinary least squares on these last 17 intervals we find our estimate of α as 2.279 with a standard error of 0.037, and R^2 = 0.997. Using the formula for the Gini coefficient on *the hypothesis of the Pareto distribution* (see page 135) we find G_Π = 1/[2×2.279-1] = 0.2811. Now, noting that the upper and lower bounds on the Gini, for incomes over $7,000, are 0.2821 and 0.2775 respectively, we find that the Pareto certainly seems to be a good fit for the last 17 income classes. Had we relied on the R^2 criterion alone, however, we might have been seriously misled, for if we reworked the calculations for all incomes above $1,000 we would still have a high R^2 (0.925) but the value of G_Π = 0.3643 lies well below the lower bound G_L = 0.4165 recorded for this group of the population in table 5-2, thus indicating that the Pareto curve is in fact a rather poor fit for all incomes above $1,000.

It seems to me that we have discovered three main hazards in the terrain covered by this section. 1 Inspection should be made of the statistical properties of the

140

estimators involved in any fitting procedure. 2 One should
check which parts of the distribution have had to be truncated in order to make the fit 'work'. 3 Care must be taken
over the 'goodness-of-fit' criterion employed. However, in
my opinion, none of these three is as hard as the less
technical problems which we encounter next.

INTERPRETING THE ANSWERS

Put yourself in the position of one who is carrying out
an independent study of inequality, or of one examining
the summary results of some recent report on the subject.
To fix ideas, let us assume that it *appears* that inequality
has decreased in the last five years. But presumably we are
not going to swallow any story received from a computer
print-out or a journal article straightaway. In this final
and important puzzle of 'colour the picture', we will do
well to question the colouring instructions which the
presentation of the facts suggests. Although the queries
that you raise in the face of the evidence may be far more
penetrating than mine, I should like to mention some basic
questions that ought to be posed, even if not satisfactorily
resolved. I shall take as understood (a) that agreement
has been reached on the definition of 'income' and other
terms and on the choice of inequality measure(s); (b) that
we are satisfied that the observed changes in inequality
are 'significant' in a statistical or formal sense as discussed in this chapter.

What cardinal representation has been used? The
retentive reader will recall from the first chapter that
two inequality measures, although *ordinally* equivalent (so
that they always rank any list of social states in the
same order), might not have equivalent *cardinal* properties,

141

so that percentage changes in inequality could appear different according to the two measures. As examples of this, take the Herfindahl index H and the coefficient of variation c. Since $H = (c^2 + 1)/n$, for the same population size H and c will always rank any pair of states in the same order. However, the relative size of any difference in inequality will be registered differently by H and by c. To see this, re-examine table 5-1 where we noted that the minimum and maximum values of c were 1.4175 and 1.5742, which means that there is a difference in measured inequality of about 10.7% which is attributable to the effect of grouping. If we did the same calculation for H, we would find that the gap appeared to be much larger, namely 14.8%. In fact H will always register larger proportional changes in inequality than c, as long as c lies above one (exactly the reverse is true for c less than one). What this implies more generally is that we should not be terribly impressed by a remark such as 'inequality has fallen by x% according to inequality measure J' unless we are quite clear in our own minds that according to some other sensible and ordinally equivalent measure the quantitative result is not substantially different[†].

Has the cake shrunk? Again you may recollect that in Chapter 1 we noted that for much of the formal work it would be necessary to take as axiomatic the existence of a fixed total of income or wealth to be shared out. This axiom is implicit in the definition of many inequality measures so that they are insensitive to changes in mean

---

[†] A technical note. It is not sufficient to normalise J so that the minimum value of J is 0, and the maximum value 1. For, suppose J does have this property, then so does J^m where m is any positive number, and of course J and J^m are ordinally, but not cardinally, equivalent.

income, and insofar as it isolates a pure distribution problem seems quite reasonable. However, presuming that society has egalitarian preferences[†], the statement 'inequality has decreased in the last five years' cannot by itself imply 'society is now in a better state' unless one is quite sure that the total to be divided has not drastically diminished also. Unless society is very averse to inequality, a mild reduction in inequality accompanied by a significant drop in average income may well be regarded as a definitely retrograde change. We can formulate this readily in the case of Atkinson's measure A_ε which is based on a social welfare function. By definition of A_ε, social welfare is an increasing function of $\bar{y}[1 - A_\varepsilon]$. Hence a drop in inequality by one per cent of its existing value will be exactly offset in social welfare terms if average income $\bar{y}$ falls by $A_\varepsilon/[1 - A_\varepsilon]$ per cent. Obviously this latter number increases with A_ε which in turn increases with ε. So, noting from the right-hand diagram in figure 5-4 that for $\varepsilon = \frac{1}{2}$, $A_{\frac{1}{2}} = 0.15$, we find that on this criterion a one per cent reduction in inequality would be exactly wiped out by a 0.18% reduction in income per head; but if $\varepsilon = 10$, $A_{10} = 0.84$, and a one per cent reduction in inequality would need to be accompanied by a $5\frac{1}{4}\%$ reduction in the cake for its effect on social welfare to be eliminated. Obviously all the remarks of this paragraph apply symmetrically to a growing cake accompanied by growing inequality.

Is the drop in inequality an optical illusion? Unfortunately this may very well be so if we have not taken carefully into consideration demographic, social and

---

† This is implied in the use of any inequality measure that satisfies the weak principle of transfers.

occupational shifts during the period. Some of these shifts you may want to include within the ambit of inequality anyway, but the treatment of others is less clear. Let us follow through two examples. Firstly, suppose there is higher inequality of earnings among doctors than among dockers, that relative remuneration and inequality within occupations have not altered over time, but that there are now relatively more dockers. Inequality in the aggregate will have decreased, although the inequality of earnings opportunity facing a new entrant to either occupation will have remained unchanged. Whether or not one concludes that inequality has 'really' gone down is in large part a matter of interpretation, though my opinion is that it has done so. I would not be so confident in the case of our second example which now follows. Suppose income inequality within age groups increases with the age of the group (this is very often true in fact). Now imagine that the age distribution is gradually shifting in favour of the young, either because the birth rate has been rising, or because pensioners are dying earlier, but that inequality within age groups remains unaltered. It will appear that inequality is falling, but this is due *entirely* to the demographic change. In fact, if your chances of physical survival are closely linked to your income, the appearance that inequality is decreasing can be quite misleading, since the death rate may have been substantially boosted by the greater inequality among the old.

There are obviously several social and economic factors which ought to be considered in a similar way. Among these are changes in the frequency of marriage and divorce, shifts (possibly cyclical) of the numbers of wives, children and other part-time or temporary workers in the labour

force, and price changes that affect people's real
incomes in different ways depending on their position in
the Parade of incomes.

How do we cope with problems of non-comparability? This
question follows naturally from the last and can be approached in two ways: non-comparability of types of income,
and non-comparability of groups of income recipients. In
the first case we may well want to examine, say, the inequality of earned income, of unearned income and the
relationship of these quantities to overall inequality.
We evidently need to have a detailed breakdown of the
income distribution both by income type and recipient –
information that is usually hard to come by. Furthermore the
mechanics of the relationship between inequality of
components of income and inequality of income as a whole are
by no means straightforward – see the appendix.

In the second case, while examining the effect of
demographic and other shifts, we may conclude that crudely
lumping together different groups of the population and thus
treating them as comparable in every way is unwarranted.
In order to handle this difficulty, it helps to have an
inequality measure that can be conveniently decomposed into
a component representing inequality within groups, and a
component giving inequality between groups. It would look
something like this:

$$J = w_1 J_1 + w_2 J_2 + w_3 J_3 + \ldots + w_k J_k + J_B$$

where J is the value of inequality in the aggregate,
$J_1, J_2, \ldots, J_k$ is the value of inequality within subgroup
1, 2, ..., k respectively, $w_1, w_2, \ldots, w_k$ form a set of
weights, and J_B is the between-group inequality, found by
assuming that everyone within a particular group has the
same income. The details of this decomposition and in

particular the specification of the weights for different
inequality measures can be found in the appendix. Given different problems of non-comparability of income recipients
there are, broadly speaking, two courses of action open to
us, each of which I shall illustrate by an example.

Firstly, suppose that each group corresponds to a particular family-size class, with the family taken as the
fundamental income-receiving unit. Then we may be able to
avoid the problem of non-comparability between groups by
adjusting incomes to an 'adult-equivalent' basis, as mentioned earlier. If the weights w depend on the shares of
each group in total income, then such an adjustment will
involve increasing the weight for a group containing small
families, decreasing the w for a group of large families.
The value of J_B would have to be recomputed for average
'per-adult equivalent' income in each group. A similar
procedure can be adopted in the case of an aggregation of
economically diverse nations within a political grouping
such as a Common Market; because of artificiality of
exchange rates or other reasons listed on page 112, average
income in each nation and thus the weights for each nation
may have to be adjusted.

In the second place, there may be little point in trying
to adjust J_B since 'between-group' inequality may be intrinsically meaningless. A case can be made for this in
examining income distributions that are differentiated by
age group. Although the measured inequality within an age
group can be seen as reflecting a genuine disparity among
people's economic prospects, the between-group component
merely reflects, for the most part, the fact that people's
incomes are not uniform over their lives. The expression
J_B may thus not reflect inequality in the conventional

146

sense at all. This being so, the problem of non-comparability
of people at different points in the lifecycle can be overcome by dropping the J_B component and adopting some alternative weighting scheme that does not involve income shares
(perhaps, for example, population shares instead) so as to
arrive at an average value of inequality over the age
groups.

Is the trend toward equality large enough to matter?
The discussion of significance in its formal, statistical
sense leaves some unsettled questions. For, all that we
glean from this technical discussion are guidelines as to
whether an apparent change in inequality could be accounted
for simply by sampling variability or by the effect of the
grouping of observations in the presentation. Whether a
reduction in inequality that passes such significance tests
is then regarded as 'important' in a wider economic or
social sense is obviously a subjective matter - it depends
on the percentage change that you happen to find personally
exciting or impressive. However, I do not think that we
have to leave the matter there. In the case of economic
inequality there are at least two ways of obtaining a crude
independent check.

The first method is to contrast the historical change
with some other easily measured inequality difference. An
interesting exercise is to compare the magnitude of the
reduction in inequality in the population as a whole during
a number of years with the change in inequality over the
life cycle as observed for the age groups in any one year.
Alternatively, one may consider the secular change in inequality alongside the apparent[†] redistribution achieved in

---

† Footnote over page

147

any one year by a major government policy instrument such as the income tax. Neither of these comparisons gives you an absolute standard of economic significance, of course, but each can certainly put a historical trend into a clear current perspective.

The second device is applicable to measures based on social welfare functions, and may be taken as an extension of the earlier shrinking-cake question. We noted there that a 1% reduction in A_ε is equivalent in social welfare terms to a $A_\varepsilon/[1-A_\varepsilon]\%$ increase in income per head. So let us suppose that for some value of ε, at the beginning of the period, $A_\varepsilon = 0.5$ (so that $A_\varepsilon/[1-A_\varepsilon] = 1$). Then if economic growth during the period raised *per capita* income by 10%, an accompanying fall of A_ε to say 0.45 would be quite impressive, since the gain to society through reduction in inequality would be as great as the benefit to society of the increase in average living standards. However, the procedure in general obviously depends on your acceptance of the social welfare function approach, and the particular result depends on the inequality-aversion which you are prepared to impute to society.

Finding and asking the right questions is an irksome task. But it is evidently a vital one too, since our brief enquiry has revealed several pitfalls which affect our under-- standing of the nature of inequality and the measurement of its extent and change. It has been persuasively argued that inequality is what economics should be all about. If this is so, then the problem of measurement becomes crucial,

---

Footnote from previous page
† The qualification 'apparent' is included because, as we noted on page 112, the observed distribution of income 'before tax' is *not* equivalent to the theoretical dist- ribution of income 'without the tax'.

and in my opinion handling numbers effectively is what measuring inequality is all about. Technical progress in calculating hardware has greatly alleviated the toil of manipulation for layman and research worker alike. So the really awkward work ahead of us is not the mechanical processing of figures. It is rather that we have to deal with figures which, instead of being docile abstractions, raise fresh challenges as we try to interpret them more carefully. However the fact that the difficulties multiply the more closely we examine the numbers should reassure us that our effort at inequality measurement is indeed worthwhile.

> 'Problems worthy
> Of attack
> Prove their worth
> By hitting back.'
>
>   - Piet Hein.

Appendix

TERMINOLOGY

The following is a list of the conventions in terminology and notation used throughout this appendix. Some further symbols are defined in table A-1.

For *discrete* distributions:

n = population size

y_i = income of man i, $i = 1, \ldots, n$

$\sum\limits_{i}$ means sum over individuals i, $i = 1, n$ (where no ambiguity is possible, i is omitted)

$\bar{y} = \dfrac{1}{n} \sum\limits_{i} y_i$ = arithmetic mean

$y^* = \exp\left(\dfrac{1}{n} \sum \log y_i\right) = [y_1 y_2 y_3 \cdots y_n]^{\frac{1}{n}}$ = geometric mean

$s_i = y_i / n\bar{y}$ = share of man i in total income.

For *continuous* distributions:

y = income

$F(y)$ = the proportion of the population with income less than or equal to y

$\int$ implies that integration is performed over the entire range of y; i.e. over $[0,\infty)$ or, equivalently for F, over the range $[0,1]$

$\bar{y} = \int y \mathrm{d}F$ = arithmetic mean income

$y^* = \exp \int \log y.\mathrm{d}F$ = geometric mean income

$\Phi(y) = \dfrac{1}{\bar{y}} \int_0^y z \mathrm{d}F(z)$ = proportion of total income received by persons who have an income less than or equal to y

$N(x) = [2\pi]^{-\frac{1}{2}} \int_{-\infty}^{x} e^{-\frac{1}{2}u^2} \mathrm{d}u$ (the standard normal distribution function, tabulated in Lindley and Miller (1966) and elsewhere).

$N^{-1}(x)$ denotes the inverse function corresponding to $N(.)$

FUNCTIONAL FORMS OF DISTRIBUTIONS

We begin this section with a simple listing of the principal properties of the lognormal and Pareto distributions in mathematical form. This is deliberately brief since a full verbal description is given in Chapter 4, and the formulas of inequality measures for these distributions are in table A-1. This table gives: 1. a general definition of each inequality measures mentioned in this book (where there are two entries, these are for the case of discrete distributions and continuous distributions, respectively); 2. the minimum value of each measure over all possible distributions; 3. the maximum possible value of each measure; 4. the formula for the measure given that the underlying distribution is lognormal; 5. the formula given that the underlying distribution is Pareto (type I).

The lognormal distribution:

$F(y) = \Lambda(y;\ \mu,\ \sigma^2) = \int_0^y \dfrac{1}{\sqrt{2\pi}\sigma x} \exp(-\dfrac{1}{2\sigma^2}[\log x - \mu]^2)\ \mathrm{d}x$

$\Phi(y) = \Lambda(y;\ \mu + \sigma^2,\ \sigma^2)$

Name	Definition	min
Variance (V)	$\frac{1}{n}\Sigma[y_i-\bar{y}]^2$	0
	$\int[y-\bar{y}]^2\,dF$	0
Coefficient of variation (c)	$\sqrt{V}/\bar{y}$	0
Range (R)	$y_{max}-y_{min}$	0
Relative mean deviation (M)	$\frac{1}{n}\Sigma\lvert y_i/\bar{y}-1\rvert$	0
	$\int\lvert y/\bar{y}-1\rvert\,dF$	0
Logarithmic variance (v)	$\frac{1}{n}\Sigma[\log(y_i/\bar{y})]^2$	0
	$\int[\log(y/\bar{y})]^2\,dF$	0
Variance of logarithms (v_1)	$\frac{1}{n}\Sigma[\log(y_i/y^\ast)]^2$	0
	$\int[\log(y/y^\ast)]^2\,dF$	0
Equal shares coefficient	$F(\bar{y})$	0
Minimal majority coefficient	$F(y_o)$, where $\Phi(y_o)=\tfrac{1}{2}$	0
Gini coefficient (concentration ratio) (G)	$\frac{1}{n^2\bar{y}}\Sigma_i\Sigma_j\lvert y_i-y_j\rvert$	0
	$1-2\int\Phi\,dF$	0

152

A-1

max	$\Lambda(y;\mu,\sigma^2)$	$\Pi(y;\underline{y},\alpha)$
$\bar{y}^2[n-1]$	$e^{2\mu+\sigma^2}[e^{\sigma^2}-1]$	$\dfrac{\alpha\, y^2}{[\alpha-1]^2\,[\alpha-2]}$
∞		
$\sqrt{[n-1]}$	$[e^{\sigma^2}-1]^{\frac{1}{2}}$	$[\alpha[\alpha-2]]^{-\frac{1}{2}}$
∞		
$n\bar{y}$		
$2[1-\frac{1}{n}]$	$2[2N(\frac{1}{2}\sigma)-1]$	$2\,\dfrac{[\alpha-1]^{\alpha-1}}{\alpha^\alpha}$
2		
∞	$\sigma^2+\frac{1}{4}\sigma^4$	$[\log\frac{\alpha-1}{\alpha}+\frac{1}{\alpha}]^2+\dfrac{1}{\alpha^2}$
∞		
∞	σ^2	$\dfrac{1}{\alpha^2}$
∞		
1	$N(\frac{1}{2}\sigma)$	$1-[\frac{\alpha-1}{\alpha}]^\alpha$
1	$N(\sigma)$	$1-2^{\frac{\alpha}{1-\alpha}}$
$\dfrac{n-1}{n}$	$2N(\sigma/\sqrt{2})-1$	$\dfrac{1}{2\alpha-1}$
1		

153

Name	Definition	min
Atkinson's Index[†] (A_ε)	$1 - \dfrac{1}{\bar{y}} \left[\Sigma \dfrac{1}{n} y_i^{1-\varepsilon} \right]^{\frac{1}{1-\varepsilon}}$	0
	$1 - \dfrac{1}{\bar{y}} \left[\int y^{1-\varepsilon}\, dF \right]^{\frac{1}{1-\varepsilon}}$	0
Dalton's Index[¶] (D_ε)	$1 - \dfrac{\Sigma\, y_i^{1-\varepsilon}}{n\,\bar{y}^{1-\varepsilon}}$	0
	$1 - \dfrac{\int y^{1-\varepsilon}\, dF}{\bar{y}^{1-\varepsilon}}$	0
Generalised Information[§] Theory Measure (I_β)	$\dfrac{1}{\beta+\beta^2} \Sigma s_i \left[s_i^\beta - n^{-\beta} \right]$	0
	$\dfrac{1}{\beta+\beta^2} \int [y/\bar{y}] \left[[y/\bar{y}]^\beta - 1 \right] dF$	0
Theil's Entropy Index (T)	$\dfrac{1}{n\bar{y}} \Sigma\, y_i\, \log(y_i/\bar{y})$	0
	$\int [y/\bar{y}] \log(y/\bar{y})\, dF$	0
Herfindahl's Index[††] (H)	$\dfrac{c^2+1}{n}$	$\dfrac{1}{n}$
	c^2+1	1

[†] This index is defined for a constant-elasticity criterion function with inequality-aversion parameter ε; $\varepsilon \geqslant 0$. The maximum value for discrete distributions applies only to the case $\varepsilon < 1$. For $\varepsilon \geqslant 1$, the maximum possible value is 1.

[¶] For $\varepsilon < 1$ only. For $\varepsilon > 1$ use $D_\varepsilon/[D_\varepsilon-1]$ which is bounded between 0 and 1. For $\varepsilon = 1$, replace the terms $y^{1-\varepsilon}$ and $\bar{y}^{1-\varepsilon}$ by $\log y$ and $\log \bar{y}$ respectively.

(contd.)

max	$\Lambda(y;\mu,\sigma^2)$	$\Pi(y;\underline{y},\alpha)$
$1 - n^{\frac{-\epsilon}{1-\epsilon}}$	$1 - e^{-\frac{1}{2}\epsilon\sigma^2}$	$1 - \frac{\alpha-1}{\alpha}\left[\frac{\alpha}{\alpha+\epsilon-1}\right]^{\frac{1}{1-\epsilon}}$
1		
$1 - n^{-\epsilon}$	$1 - e^{-\frac{1}{2}\sigma^2\epsilon[1-\epsilon]}$	$1 - \frac{\alpha}{\alpha+\epsilon-1}\left[\frac{\alpha-1}{\alpha}\right]^{1-\epsilon}$
1		
$\frac{1-n^{-\beta}}{\beta+\beta^2}$ ∞	$\frac{1}{\beta+\beta^2}\left[e^{\frac{1}{2}\sigma^2[\beta+\beta^2]}-1\right]$	$\frac{\frac{\alpha}{\alpha-\beta-1}\left[\frac{\alpha-1}{\alpha}\right]^{\beta+1}-1}{\beta+\beta^2}$
$\log n$ ∞	$\frac{1}{2}\sigma^2$	$\frac{1}{\alpha-1} - \log\frac{\alpha}{\alpha-1}$
1 ∞	e^{σ^2}	$\frac{[\alpha-1]^2}{\alpha[\alpha-2]}$

§ In the discrete case, the maximum value is $\log n$ when $\beta = 0$, and is ∞ when $\beta < -1$.

†† Notice that a slightly different formulation must be adopted in the case of the continuous distribution. This is identical, however, to a cardinally equivalent transformation of the discrete definition (for a given population).

155

$$\bar{y} = e^{\mu + \frac{1}{2}\sigma^2}$$

$$y* = e^{\mu}$$

Lorenz curve: $\Phi = N(N^{-1}(F) - \sigma)$.

The Pareto distribution (type I):

$$F(y) = \Pi(y; \underline{y}, \alpha) = 1 - [\underline{y}/y]^{\alpha}$$

$$\Phi(y) = \Pi(y; \underline{y}, \alpha-1)$$

$$\bar{y} = \frac{\alpha}{\alpha-1}\underline{y}$$

$$y* = e^{1/\alpha}\underline{y}$$

Lorenz curve: $\Phi = 1 - [1-F]^{1-1/\alpha}$

The last equation may be used to give a straightforward interpolation formula for observed points on a Lorenz curve. Given two such observed points (F_0, Φ_0), (F_1, Φ_1), then for an arbitrary intermediate value F (so that $F_0 < F < F_1$), the corresponding intermediate Φ-value is:

$$\Phi = 1 - [1-\Phi_0]\ \exp\left(\frac{\log\frac{1-F}{1-F_0}\ \log\frac{1-\Phi_1}{1-\Phi_0}}{\log\frac{1-F_1}{1-F_0}}\right)$$

However if this formula is used to interpolate between observed points when the underlying distribution is not Pareto type I then the following difficulty may arise. Suppose the class intervals used in grouping the data $\{a_1, a_2, a_3, \ldots, a_k, a_{k+1}\}$, the proportions of the population in each group $\{f_1, f_2, f_3, \ldots, f_k\}$, and the average income of each group $\{\mu_1, \mu_2, \mu_3, \ldots, \mu_k\}$, are all known. Then, as described on page 128, a 'maximum inequality' Lorenz curve may be drawn through the observed points using this information. However the above Pareto interpolation formula does *not* use the information on the *a*s, and the resulting interpolated Lorenz curve may cross the maximum inequality curve. The following method, which fits a Pareto type I density function within each interval, avoids this difficulty and has been used to calculate 'compromise' values of inequality measures in Chapter 5. Write $\underline{y}^{\alpha}$ as A, so that the Pareto density function becomes $f(y) = \alpha A y^{-1-\alpha}$. Using the above information, the values of the parameters A, α *for the particular interval* (a_i, a_{i+1}) can be found from the equations:

$$f_i = A \left[a_i^{-\alpha} - a_{i+1}^{-\alpha} \right]$$

$$\mu_i = \frac{\alpha}{\alpha-1} A \left[a_i^{1-\alpha} - a_{i+1}^{1-\alpha} \right]$$

which may be solved by computer program. Call these solutions A_i, α_i. Having performed this operation for each interval we may write equation (3) on page 120

$$J = \sum_{i=1}^{k} \int_{a_i}^{a_{i+1}} h(y) \alpha_i A_i y^{-1-\alpha_i} \, dy$$

Interpolation on the Lorenz curve may be done as follows. Between the observations i and $i+1$ the interpolated values of F and Φ are

$$F(y) = F_i + A_i \left[a_i^{-\alpha_i} - y^{-\alpha_i} \right]$$

$$\Phi(y) = \Phi_i + \frac{\alpha_i A_i}{\alpha_i - 1} \left[a_i^{1-\alpha_i} - y^{1-\alpha_i} \right]$$

As noted in Chapter 4 many functional forms have been used other than the lognormal and the Pareto. Since there is not the space to discuss these in the same detail, the remainder of this section simply deals with the main types; indicating family relationships, and giving the moments

about zero where possible. (If you have the rth moment
about zero, then many other inequality measures are easily
calculated; for example $A_\varepsilon = 1 - [[\mu_r']^{1/r}]/\mu_1'$, where μ_r'
is the rth moment about zero, $r = 1-\varepsilon$ and $\mu_1' = \bar{y}$.)

We deal first with family relations of the Pareto distribution. In its most general form, known as the type III
Pareto distribution, we may write the distribution function
as

$$F(y) = 1 - e^{-ky} [\gamma + \delta y]^{-\alpha}$$

where k, $\gamma \geqslant 0$, and α, $\delta > 0$. By putting $k = 0$ in the above
equation we obtain the Pareto type II distribution. By
putting $\gamma = 0$ and $\delta = 1/\underline{y}$ in the type II distribution we
get the Pareto type I distribution, $\Pi(y; \underline{y}, \alpha)$.

Singh and Maddala (1976) suggested as a useful functional form the following general distribution:

$$F(y) = 1 - [\gamma + \delta y^\beta]^{-\alpha}$$

where α, β, γ, δ are parameters such that $F(0) = 0$, $F(\infty) = 1$,
and $F'(y) = f(y) \geqslant 0$. From this we can derive the following
special cases.

(i)   If $\beta = 1$ we have the Pareto type II distribution.

(ii)   If $\gamma = 1$, $\delta = \frac{1}{\alpha} k^\beta$ and $\alpha \to \infty$ then the so-called
Weibull distribution is generated: $F(y) = 1 - \exp(-[ky]^\beta)$.
The rth moment about zero is given by $\mu_r' = k^{-r}\Gamma(1+r/\beta)$,
where $\Gamma(x)$ is the so-called Gamma function defined as
$\int_0^\infty u^x e^{-u}\, du$.

(iii)   A special case of the Weibull may be found when
$\beta = 1$, namely the exponential distribution $F(y) = 1 -$
$\exp(-ky)$. Moments are given by $k^{-r}\Gamma(1+r)$ which for integral
values of r is simply $k^{-r}\, r!$.

(iv)   If $\alpha = \gamma = 1$ and $\delta = \underline{y}^{-\beta}$, then we find Fisk's sech^2-distribution: $F(y) = 1 - [1+ [y/\underline{y}]^\beta]^{-1}$, with the rth

moment about zero given by $\mu'_r = r\underline{y}^r \frac{\pi}{\beta}/ \sin(\frac{r\pi}{\beta})$ where

$- \beta < r < \beta$. Furthermore the upper tail of the distribution
is asymptotic to a conventional Pareto type I distribution
with parameters $\underline{y}$ and β (for low values of y the distribution approximates to a reverse Pareto distribution - see
Fisk, p.175). The distribution gets its name from the transformation $[y/\underline{y}]^\beta = e^x$, whence the transformed density
function is $f(x) = e^x /[1+e^x]^2$, which is a special case of
the logistic function.

The sech^2 distribution can also be found as a special
case of the Champernowne distribution:

$$F(y) = 1 - \frac{1}{\theta} \tan^{-1} \left(\frac{\sin\theta}{\cos\theta + [y/\underline{y}]^\beta} \right) ,$$

where θ is a parameter lying between $-\pi$ and π (see
Champernowne, 1952; Fisk, 1961). This likewise approximates
the Pareto type I distribution in its upper tail and has
the following moments about zero:

$$\mu'_r = \underline{y}^r \frac{\pi}{\theta} \sin(\frac{r\theta}{\beta}) / \sin(\frac{r\pi}{\beta}), \quad - \beta < r < \beta .$$

The required special case is found by letting $\theta \to 0$.

The so-called Yule distribution can be written either
in general form with density function

$$f(y) = A B_\nu(y,\rho+1),$$

where $B_\nu(y, \rho+1)$ is the incomplete Beta function
$\int_0^\nu u^{y-1}[1-u]^\rho du$, $\rho > 0$ and $0 < \nu \leqslant 1$, or in its special
form with $\nu = 1$, where the frequency is then proportional
to the complete Beta function $B(y, \rho+1)$.[†] Its moments are

---

† The Beta and Gamma functions are extensively tabulated.
Their analytical properties are discussed in many texts on
statistics, for example Keeping (1962), Weatherburn (1949).

$$\mu'_r = \sum_{i=1}^{n} \frac{\rho n!}{\rho - n} \Delta_{n,r} \quad \text{for } \rho > r, \text{ where}$$

$$\Delta_{n,r} = [-1]^{r-n} \sum_{i=1}^{n} \sum_{j=i}^{n} \sum_{k=j}^{n} \dots [\,ijk\dots] \quad \text{if } n < r$$

$$\underbrace{\phantom{\sum_{i=1}^{n} \sum_{j=i}^{n} \sum_{k=j}^{n}}}_{(r-n \text{ terms})}$$

$$= 1 \qquad\qquad\qquad\qquad \text{if } n = r$$

The Yule distribution in its special form approximates the distribution $\Pi(y; \Gamma(\rho)^{1/\rho}, \rho)$ in its upper tail. A further interesting property of this special form is that for a *discrete* variable it satisfies van der Wijk's law.

We now turn to a rich family of distributions of which two members have been used to some extent in the study of income distribution – the Pearson curves. The Pearson type I is the Beta distribution with density function:

$$f(y) = y^{\xi} [1-y]^{\eta} / B(\xi,\eta), \qquad 0 < y < 1^{\dagger}$$

where ξ, $\eta > 0$. The rth moment about zero can be written $B(\xi+r,\eta)/B(\xi,\eta)$ or as $\Gamma(\xi+r)\Gamma(\xi+\eta)/[\Gamma(\xi)\Gamma(\xi+\eta+r)]$. The Gamma distribution is of the type III of the Pearson family:

$$f(y) = \frac{\lambda^{\phi}}{\Gamma(\phi)} y^{\phi-1} e^{-\lambda y},$$

where λ, $\phi > 0$. The moments are given by

$$\mu'_r = \lambda^{-r} \Gamma(\phi+r) / \Gamma(\phi).$$

Three interesting properties of the Gamma function are as follows. Firstly, by putting $\phi = 1$, we find that it has

---

† This restriction means that y must be normalised by dividing it by its assumed maximum value.

the exponential distribution as a special case. Secondly, suppose that $\lambda = 1$, and that y has the Gamma distribution with $\phi = \phi_1$ while w has the Gamma distribution with $\phi = \phi_2$. Then the sum $w + y$ also has the Gamma distribution with $\phi = \phi_1 + \phi_2$: a property that is obviously useful if one is considering, say, the decomposition of income into con-stituent parts such as earned and unearned income. Thirdly, a Beta distribution with a high parameter η looks very similar to a Gamma distribution with high values of para-meters λ, ϕ. This can be seen from the formula for the moments. For high values of x and any constant k it is the case that $\Gamma(x) / \Gamma(x+k) \simeq x^{-k}$. Hence the moments of the B-distribution approximate to $[\xi+\eta]^{-r} \Gamma(\xi+r) / \Gamma(\xi)$.

The relationships mentioned in the previous paragraphs are set out in table A-2. Solid arrows indicate that one distribution is a special case of another. Dotted lines indicate that for high values of the income variable and/ or for certain parameter values, one distribution closely approximates another.

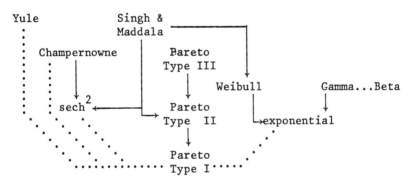

Table A-2

Finally let us look at distributions related to the log-normal. The most obvious is the three-parameter lognormal which is defined as follows. If $y - \tau$ has the distribution $\Lambda(\mu,\sigma^2)$ where τ is some parameter, then y has the three-parameter lognormal distribution with parameters τ, μ, σ^2. The moments about zero are difficult to calculate analytically, although the moments about $y = \tau$ are obviously easy: $\int [y-\tau]^r \, dF(y) = \exp(r\mu + \frac{1}{2}r^2\sigma^2)$. Certain inequality measures can be written down without much difficulty - see Aitchison and Brown (1959, p. 15). Also note that the lognormal distribution is related indirectly to the Yule distribution: a certain class of stochastic processes which is of interest in several fields of economics has as its limiting distribution either the lognormal or the Yule distribution, depending on the restrictions placed upon the process. On this see Simon and Bonini (1958).

PROPERTIES OF A_ε AND D_ε

We have $A_\varepsilon = 1 - [\frac{1}{n} \Sigma_i \, [y_i/\bar{y}]^{1-\varepsilon}]^{1/1-\varepsilon}$. Rearranging this and differentiating with respect to ε, one obtains:

$$\log(1-A_\varepsilon) + \frac{1-\varepsilon}{1-A_\varepsilon} \frac{\partial A_\varepsilon}{\partial \varepsilon} = \frac{\Sigma [y_i/\bar{y}]^{1-\varepsilon} \log(y_i/\bar{y})}{\Sigma [y_i/\bar{y}]^{1-\varepsilon}}$$

Define $x_i = [y_i/\bar{y}]^{1-\varepsilon}$. Noting that $y_i \geqslant 0$ implies $x_i \geqslant 0$ and that $\bar{x} = \frac{1}{n} \Sigma \, x_i = [1-A_\varepsilon]^{1-\varepsilon}$, we may derive the following result:

$$\frac{\partial A_\varepsilon}{\partial \varepsilon} = \left[\frac{\bar{x}[1-A_\varepsilon]}{[1-\varepsilon]^2}\right] \left[\frac{1}{n} \Sigma x_i \, \log x_i - \bar{x} \, \log \bar{x}\right].$$

We see immediately that the first term on the right hand side cannot be negative, since $\bar{x} \geqslant 0$ and $0 \leqslant A_\varepsilon \leqslant 1$. Now it may be checked that $x \log x$ is a convex function so that

162

the second term on the right hand side is non-negative. Thus $\partial A_\varepsilon / \partial \varepsilon \geq 0$ and so A_ε *never* decreases with ε for any income distribution. Now consider D_ε; we find that if $\varepsilon \neq 1$:

$$\frac{\partial D_\varepsilon}{\partial \varepsilon} = [\, 1 - D_\varepsilon\,][\, \log(1 - A_\varepsilon) + \frac{1 - \varepsilon}{1 - A_\varepsilon}\,]\ .$$

If $0 \leq \varepsilon < 1$ the second term on the right hand side may be positive, zero or negative since $\log(1 - A_\varepsilon) \leq 0$. Hence D_ε may increase or decrease with ε, even if $0 \leq D_\varepsilon \leq 1$.

PROPERTIES OF v AND v_1

Consider the inequality measure $\frac{1}{n} \sum [\, \log(y_i / a)]^2$, where a is some arbitrary positive number. The change in inequality resulting from a transfer of a small amount of income from man j to man i is:

$$\frac{2}{n y_i} \log(y_i / a) - \frac{2}{n y_j} \log(y_j / a) + \frac{2}{n a} \left[\frac{\partial a}{\partial y_i} - \frac{\partial a}{\partial y_j} \right] \sum \log(y_k / a)\ .$$

If $a = \bar{y}$ (the case of the measure v) then $\partial a / \partial y_i = \partial a / \partial y_j$ and so the last term is zero. If $a = y^*$ (the case of the measure v_1), then $\sum \log(y_k) = n \log(a)$, and once again the last term is zero. Hence we see that for v and v_1 the sign of the above expression depends entirely on the behaviour of the function $\frac{1}{x} \log x$, which occurs in the first two terms. Now the first derivative of this function is $[1 - \log x] / x^2$, which is positive or negative as $x \lessgtr e = 2.71828 \dots$

Suppose $y_i > y_j$. Then as long as $y_i \leq ae$, we see that because $\frac{1}{x} \log x$ is an increasing function under these conditions, the effect of the above transfer is to increase inequality (as we would require under the principle of transfers). However, if $y_j \geq ae$, then exactly the reverse conclusions apply – the above transfer effect is negative. Note that in this argument a may be taken to be $\bar{y}$ or y^*

163

according as the measure under consideration is v or v_1.

VAN DER WIJK'S LAW

1. First we shall derive the average income $\theta(y)$ of everyone above an income level y. This is

$$\theta(y) = \int_y^\infty uf(u)\,du / \int_y^\infty f(u)\,du .$$

$$= \bar{y}[\,1-\Phi(y)]\,/[\,1-F(y)]$$

From the above, for the Pareto distribution we have

$$\theta(y) = \frac{\alpha}{\alpha-1}\, \underline{y}\, [\,\underline{y}/y]^{\alpha-1}\, [\,\underline{y}/y]^{-\alpha}$$

$$= \frac{\alpha}{\alpha-1}\, y .$$

Hence average income above the level y is proportional to y itself.

2. I now show that this result is true only for the Pareto distribution within the class of continuous distributions. Letting $\theta(y) = \gamma y$ where γ is a constant and rearranging, we have

$$\int_y^\infty uf(u)\,du = \gamma y \int_y^\infty f(u)\,du,$$

Where $f(y)$ is of course unknown. Differentiate this with respect to y:

$$-y\, f(y) = -\gamma yf(y) + \gamma[\,1-F(y)]$$

Define $\alpha = \gamma/[\,\gamma-1]$, then rearranging this equation, we have

$$yf(y) + \alpha F(y) = \alpha .$$

Since $f(y) = dF(y)/dy$, this can be treated as a differential equation in y. Solving for F, we have

$$y^\alpha F(y) = y^\alpha + B$$

where B is a constant. Since $F = 0$ when $y = \underline{y}$, we have $B = -\underline{y}^\alpha$.

164

So

$$F(y) = 1 - [\underline{y}/y]^{\alpha}$$

Q.E.D.

THE DECOMPOSITION OF INEQUALITY MEASURES

Certain inequality measures lend themselves readily to an analysis of inequality within and between groups in the population. Let there be k such groups so arranged that every member of the population belongs to one and only one group, and let the proportion of the population falling in group j be g_j; obviously $\Sigma_{j=1}^{k} g_j = 1$. Write mean income in group j as $\bar{y}_j$, and the share of group j in total income as S_j, so that $S_j = g_j \bar{y}_j / \bar{y}$ and $\Sigma_{j=1}^{k} g_j \bar{y}_j = \bar{y}$ and $\Sigma_{j=1}^{k} S_j = 1$. In what follows, the first term on the right hand side of each equation is the within-group component of inequality and consists of a weighted sum of inequality measures calculated for each group as if it were a population in its own right; the inequality measure for group j considered on its own is indicated by a subscript j. The second term (where present) is the between-group component of inequality, and is indicated by a subscript B; to calculate this, simply assume that everyone within a group receives that group's mean income.

The decomposition is particularly easy for the family of measures I_β derived from information theory:

$$I_\beta = \sum_{j=1}^{k} S_j^{\beta+1} I_{\beta j} + I_{\beta B}$$

It is evident that the set of weights $S_j^{\beta+1}$ used in forming the within-group component will only add up to 1 if $\beta=0$ in which case of course we have Theil's measure:

165

$$T = \sum_{j=1}^{k} S_j T_j + T_B$$

The other important special case is $\beta = 1$. Recalling that $I_1 = \frac{1}{2}[H-1/n]$, where H is the Herfindahl index, we have:

$$H = \sum_{j=1}^{k} S_j^2 H_j$$

Unfortunately, Atkinson's measure A_ε, although ordinally equivalent to I_β for $\beta < 0$, does not decompose quite so neatly. The formula is:

$$A_\varepsilon = 1 - \left[\sum_{j=1}^{k} \left[g_j [\bar{y}_j / \bar{y}]^{1-\varepsilon} [1 - A_{\varepsilon j}]^{1-\varepsilon} \right] \right]^{1/1-\varepsilon}$$

The variance V and the variance of logarithms v_1 each decomposes very conveniently:

$$V = \sum_{j=1}^{k} g_j V_j + V_B ,$$

$$v_1 = \sum_{j=1}^{k} g_j v_{1j} + v_{1B}$$

although in the calculation of v_{1B} one needs to assume that everyone within group j receives the geometric mean income within the group rather than the arithmetic mean.

Finally, consider the problem of decomposition of inequality measures *by component of income* rather than by population subgroup. For simplicity suppose there are two such components A and B so that y_{iA} and y_{iB} are, respectively, the amounts of A-income and B-income received by man i; so of course $y_i = y_{iA} + y_{iB}$. Similarly define $\bar{y}_A = \frac{1}{n} \Sigma_i y_{iA}$ and $\bar{y}_B = \frac{1}{n} \Sigma_i y_{iB}$, and for a given mean-independent

166

inequality measure J let J_T be total inequality, J_A the inequality of A-income alone, and J_B the inequality of B-income. Consider, for convenience, the special case[†] where J may be written:

$$J = \Psi\left(\frac{1}{n}\sum_{i=1}^{n}\psi(y_i/\bar{y})\right)$$

(Note the similarity to equation (2) on page 115. The function $h(y)$ has been rewritten $\psi(y/\bar{y})$, and, if the function Ψ is increasing, it represents an ordinally equivalent transformation).

If the function $\psi(.)$ is convex (so that its first derivative never decreases), $\frac{1}{n}\sum\psi(y_i/\bar{y})$ itself is an inequality measure satisfying the weak principle of transfers. As long as $\Psi(.)$ is convex the following relationship holds:

$$J_T \leqslant \frac{\bar{y}_A}{\bar{y}}\ J_A + \frac{\bar{y}_B}{\bar{y}}\ J_B \ .$$

In other words, for such an inequality measure, total inequality does not exceed the weighted average of inequality of each income component, where the proportions of A-income and B-income are used as weights. Note that if Ψ is not convex, the result will not hold. As it happens all the measures cited in table A-1, except V, v and v_1 will satisfy the above inequality.

---

† More generally we require that J be a convex function of the vector of income shares.

Notes on the literature

These notes cite the sources which have been used for the discussion in the text and provide a guide for further reading. In addition some more recondite supplementary points are mentioned. The arrangement follows the order of the material in the five chapters.

CHAPTER 1

Notes. A useful general discussion of conventional terminology and approach is found in Prest and Bauer (1973); reference may also be made to the first chapter of Atkinson (1975) and Chapter 2 of Thurow (1975).

The issue of the measurability of the income concept is taken up in a very readable contribution by Boulding (1975), as are several other basic questions about the meaning of the subject which were raised by the nine interpretations cited in the text. For an introduction to the formal analysis of measurability and comparability, see Sen (1973, pp. 43-46), and perhaps then try going on to Sen (1974), which although harder is clearly expounded. There are several studies which use an attribute other than income or wealth, and which provide interesting material for comparison: Jencks (1973) puts income inequality in the much wider context of social inequality; Addo (1976) considers international inequality in such things as school enrolment, calorie consumption, energy consumption and numbers of physicians; Alker (1965) discusses a quantification of voting power; Russet (1964) relates inequality in land ownership to political instability. The problem of the size of the cake depending on the way it is cut has long been implicitly recognised (for example, in the optimal taxation literature) but does not feature prominently in the works on inequality measurement. For a general treatment read Tobin (1970), reprinted in Phelps (1973) and then if you can manipulate the mathematics, go on to the other papers in Phelps. On this see also Okun's (1975, Chapter 4) illustration of 'leaky bucket' income transfers.

On some of the classical principles of justice and equality, see Rees (1971), Chapter 7, Wilson (1966). A notable landmark in modern thought is Rawls (1972) which, depending on the manner of interpretation of the principles of justice there expounded, implies most specific recommendations for comparing unequal allocations. Bowen (1970) introduces the concept of 'minimum practicable inequality', which incorporates the idea of special personal merit in determining a just allocation. The question of the relationship between inequality in the whole population and inequality in subgroups of the population with reference to heterogeneity due to age is tackled in Paglin (1975) and in Cowell (1975). The rather technical paper of Champernowne (1974) explores the relationship between measures of inequality as a whole and measures that are related specifically to low incomes, middle incomes, or to high incomes. Stark's (1972) approach to an equality index is based on a head-count measure of poverty, and is discussed in the next chapter. Batchelder (1971, page 30) discusses the 'poverty gap' approach to the measurement of poverty. The link between a measure that captures the depth of poverty and the Gini index of inequality (see Chapter 2) is analysed in Sen (1976), which unfortunately the general reader will find quite hard.

CHAPTER 2

Notes. One often finds that technical apparatus or analytical results that have become associated with some famous name were introduced years before by someone else in some dusty journal but were never popularised. So it is with Pen's Parade, set out in Pen (1974), which had been anticipated by Schutz (1951), and only rarely used since – Cf. Budd (1970). As we have seen, the Parade is simply related to the cumulative frequency distribution if you turn the piece of paper over once you have drawn the diagram. To find out

more about this concept, and also frequency distributions
and histograms, consult any good introductory statistics
text such as Allen (1949), Connor and Morrell (1964) or
Keeping (1962). For a formal exposition of the Lorenz curve
and proof of the assertions made in the text see Levine and
Singer (1970) and Gastwirth (1971).

The famous concentration ratio – Gini (1912) – also has
an obscure precursor. Thirty six years before Gini's work,
F.R. Helmert discussed the ordinally equivalent measure
known as Gini's mean difference – for further information
see David (1968). The process of rediscovering old
implements left lying around in the inequality-analyst's
toolshed continues unabated, so that often several labels
and descriptions exist for essentially the same concept.
Hence M, the relative mean deviation, used by Schutz (1951),
Dalton (1920) and Kuznets (1959), reappears as the maximum
equalisation percentage, which is exactly $\frac{1}{2}M$ (see United
Nations, 1957), and as the 'standard average difference'
(Francis, 1972). Eltetö and Frigyes produce three measures
which are closely related to M, and Addo's 'systemic
inequality measure' is essentially a function of these
related measures. See also Kondor (1971).

The properties of the more common *ad hoc* inequality
measures are discussed at length in Atkinson (1970, pp.
252-257; 1973, pp. 53-58), Champernowne (1974, pp. 805) and
Sen (1973, pp. 24-36). The use of the skewness statistic was
proposed by Young (1917), and this and other statistical
moments are considered further by Champernowne (1974).
Further details on the use of moments may be found in texts
such as Keeping. For more on the minimal majority coefficient
(sometimes known as the Dauer-Kelsay index of malapportion-
ment) see Alker and Russet (1964), Alker (1965) and Davis
(1954, pp. 138-143). Some of the criticisms of Stark's high/
low measure are raised in Polanyi and Wood (1974). Another
such practical measure with a similar flavour is Wiles'
(1974) semi-decile ratio: (Minimum income of top 5%)/
(maximum income of bottom 5%). One immediately notes that,
like M, 'minimal majority', 'equal shares', and 'high/low',
this measure is insensitive to certain transfers, notably
in the middle income ranges (you can redistribute income
from a man at the sixth percentile to a man at the ninety-
fourth without changing the semi-decile ratio). In my
opinion this is a serious weakness, but Wiles thinks that
the semi-decile ratio focuses on the essential feature of
income inequality to the exclusion of others.

Wiles and Markowski argue for a presentation of the
facts about inequality that captures the whole distribution,
since conventional inequality measures are a type of

sophisticated average, and 'the average is a very uniform-
ative concept' (1971, p. 351). In this respect[†] their
appeal is similar in spirit to that of Sen (1973, Chapter
3) who suggests using the Lorenz curve to rank income
distributions in a 'quasi-ordering' - in other words a
ranking where the arrangement of some of the items is
ambiguous. The method of percentiles is used extensively
by Lydall (1959) and Polanyi and Wood. The formalisation
of this approach as a 'comparative function' was suggested
by Esberger and Malmquist.

CHAPTER 3

Notes. The 'traditional' view of social welfare functions is
admirably and concisely expounded in Graaff. One of the
principal difficulties with these functions, as with the
physical universe, is - where do they come from? On this
technically difficult question, see Sen (1970) and Mayston
(1974). If you are sceptical about the practical usefulness
of SWFs you may wish to note some other areas of applied
economics where SWFs similar to those discussed in the text
have been employed. They are introduced to derive interpersonal weights in applications of cost-benefit analysis,
and in particular into project appraisal in developing
countries (cf. Dasgupta and Pearce, 1972, Chapter 2, and
Little and Mirrlees, 1974, Chapter 3). A SWF may be applied
to evaluate the distributional effects of regional policy
(Brown, 1972, pp. 81-84), and an implicit SWF may be used to
determine the distributional intentions of tax legislation -
Mera (1969). Even gross national product statistics may be
regarded as the evaluation of a simple kind of SWF.
    For the relationship of SWFs to inequality measurement,
either in general form, or the specific type mentioned
here, see Sen (1973), Atkinson (1974, p. 63; 1975, pp. 45-
49). The association of Rawls' (1972) concept of justice
(where society gives priority to improving the position of
the least advantaged person) with a SWF exhibiting extreme
inequality aversion is discussed in Sen (1974, pp. 395-398),
Arrow (1973) and Hammond (1975). Inequality measures of the
type first suggested by Dalton (1920) are further discussed
by Aigner and Heins (1967) and Bentzel (1970). Kolm (1976)
suggests a measure based on an alternative to assumption 5,

---

† But only in this respect, since they reject the Lorenz
  curve as an 'inept choice', preferring to use histograms
  instead.

namely constant *absolute* inequality aversion, so that as
we increase a man's income y by one unit (pound, dollar,
etc.) his welfare weight U' drops by $\alpha\%$ where α is the
constant amount of absolute inequality aversion. In
general this approach leads to an inequality measure which
does not satisfy the principle of scale independence. He
also suggests a measure generalising both this and
Atkinson's measure. The SWF method is interpreted by Meade
(1976, Chapter 7 and appendix) in a more blatantly
utilitarian fashion; his measure of 'proportionate
distributional waste' is based on an estimation of
individual utility functions.

The proofs of theorems 1 and 2 using slightly more
restrictive assumptions than necessary were established in
Atkinson (1970) who drew heavily on an analogy involving
probability theory. Versions of the theorems requiring
weaker assumptions but fairly sophisticated mathematics are
found in Dasgupta, Sen and Starrett (1973), Kolm (1969) and
Sen (1973, pp. 49-58). Types of permissibly 'distance'
function, and their relationship with inequality is
discussed in Cowell and Kuga (1976); Love and Wolfson (1976)
refer to a similar concept as the 'strength-of-transfer
effect'. The special relationship of the Herfindahl index
and the Theil index to the strong principle of transfers was
first examined in Kuga (1973).

Herfindahl's (1950) measure (which is obviously closely
related to c^2, or to Francis' standard average square
difference) was originally suggested as a measure of
concentration of individual firms – see Rosenbluth (1955).
Several other inequality measures can be used in this way,
notably other members of the I_β family. The variable
corresponding to income y may then be taken to be a firm's
sales. However, one needs to be careful about this analogy
since inequality among persons and concentration among
firms are rather different concepts in several important
ways: (i) the definition of a firm is often unclear,
particularly for small production units; (ii) in measuring
concentration we may not be very worried about the presence
of tiny sales shares of many small firms, whereas in
measuring inequality we may be considerably perturbed by
tiny incomes received by a lot of people – see Hannah and
Kay (1977).

A reworking of the information theory analogy leads us
to a closely related class of measures that satisfy the
strong principle of transfers, but where the average of the
distance of actual incomes from inequality is found by using
population shares rather than income shares as weights,

thus:

$$\frac{1}{\beta} \sum_{i=1}^{n} \frac{1}{n} \left[h(s_i) - h(\frac{1}{n}) \right]$$

- cf. expression (6) in the text. The special case $\beta=0$ which becomes $\Sigma \log(\bar{y}/y_i)/n$ is discussed in Theil (1967, Chapter 4 and appendix). An ordinally equivalent variant of expression (1), Theil's measure, is used in Marfels (1971).

The social value judgments implied by the use of the various *ad hoc* inequality measures in Chapters 2 and 3 are analysed in Kondor (1975) who extends the discussion in the works of Atkinson, Champernowne and Sen cited in the notes to Chapter 2. The question of what happens to inequality measures when all incomes are increased or when the population is replicated or merged with another population is discussed in Kolm (1976). In particular theorem 2 can be extended. Suppose we have a measure that registers higher inequality if all incomes are increased in proportion, and that distribution A (with high total income) has a Lorenz curve that lies below that of distribution B (with a low total); then if the weak principle of transfers holds, A registers greater inequality than does B.

CHAPTER 4

Notes. Almost any sound text on introductory statistical theory will give an introduction to the normal distribution - for example Keeping (1962) or Mood and Graybill (1962). For the less mathematically inclined reader a more tender treatment is given in Reichmann (1961) or Hoel (1966). The standard reference on the lognormal and its properties Aitchison and Brown (1957) also contains a succinct account of a simple type of random process theory of income development. A summary of several such theories can be found in Bronfenbrenner (1971) and in Brown (1976). On some of the properties of the lognormal Lorenz curve, see also Aitchison and Brown (1954).

Pareto's original work can be consulted in Pareto (1965) or in Pareto (1972), which deals in passing with some of Pareto's late views on the law of income distribution. Tawney (1964) argues forcefully against the strict inter-pretation of Pareto's Law. 'It implies a misunderstanding of the nature of economic laws in general, and of Pareto's laws in particular, at which no one, it is probable, would have been more amused than Pareto himself, and which, indeed, he expressly repudiated in a subsequent work. It is to believe in economic Fundamentalism, with the New Testament left out, and the Books of Leviticus and Deuteronomy inflated to unconscionable proportions by the addition of new and appalling chapters. It is to dance naked, and roll on the ground, and cut oneself with knives, in honour of the mysteries of Mumbo Jumbo.' However I do not find his assertion of Pareto's recantation convincing - see Pareto (1972); see also Pigou, (1952, pp. 650 ff.). Unfortunately, oversimplified interpretations of the Law persist - Adams suggests a 'golden section' value of $\alpha = 2/[\sqrt{5}-1]$ as a cure for inflation. Van der Wijk's (1939) law is partially discussed in Pen (1974, Chapter 6). Several of the other results in the text are formally proved in Chipman (1975). Nicholson (1969, pp. 286-292) and Bowman (1945) give a simple account of the use of the Pareto diagram.

Recent evidence on the suitability of the Pareto and lognormal distributions as approximations to actual distributions of earnings and of income can be found in the Royal Commission on the Distribution of Income and Wealth (1975, Appendix C; 1976, Appendix E). Bjerke (1970) dealing with the structure of wages in Copenhagen in 1953 shows that the more homogenous the occupation, the more likely it would be that the distribution of earnings within it was lognormal. Hill (1959) shows that merging normal distributions with different variances leads to a 'leptokurtosis' (more of the population in the 'tails' than expected from a normal distribution) - typical feature of the distribution of the logarithm of income. Other useful references on the lognormal distribution in practice are Fase (1970), Takahashi (1959), Thatcher (1968). Atkinson (1975a) and Soltow (1975) produce evidence on the Pareto distribution and the distribution of wealth in the UK and the USA of the 1860's respectively.

For further evidence on the variability of Pareto's α in the USA, see Johnson (1937), a cautious supporter of Pareto. Some of the less orthodox applications of the Pareto curve are in Zipf (1949). Harold T. Davis, who has become famous for his theory of the French Revolution in terms of the value of Pareto's α under Louis XVI, produces further evidence on the Pareto Law in terms of the distribution of wealth in the pre-Civil War southern states (wealth measured in terms of number of slaves) and of the distribution of income in England under William the Conqueror - see Davis (1954). For the latter example (based on the Domesday Book, 1086) the fit is surprisingly good, even though income is measured in 'acres' - i.e. that area of land which produced $7\frac{1}{2}$ bushels of wheat *per annum*. The

174

population covered includes Cotters, Serfs, Villeins, Sokemen, Freemen, Tenants, Lords and Nobles, Abbots, Bishops, the Bishop of Bayeux, the Count of Mortain, and of course King William himself.

However, Davis' (1941) interpretation of these and other intrinsically interesting historical excursions as evidence for a 'mathematical theory of history' seems mildly bizarre: supposedly if α is too low or too high a revolution (from the left or the right, respectively) is induced. Although there is clearly a connection between extreme economic inequality and social unrest, seeking the mainspring of the development of civilisation in the slope of a line on a double-log graph does not appear to be a rewarding or convincing exercise. There is a similar danger in misinterpreting a dynamic model such as the of Champernowne (1953), in which a given pattern of social mobility always produces, eventually, a unique Pareto distribution, independent of the income distribution originally prevailing. Bernadelli (1944) postulates that a revolution having redistribution as an aim will prove futile because of such a mathematical process. Finding the logical and factual holes in this argument is left as an exercise for you.

Finally, we cite references for other functional forms which are claimed to fit observed distributions more or less satisfactorily and which are discussed in the appendix. Some are generalisations of the lognormal or Pareto forms, such as the three-parameter lognormal – Metcalf (1969) – or the generalised Pareto-Levy law, which attempts to take account of the lower tail – Mandelbrot (1960). Indeed, note that the formula we have described as *the* Pareto distribution was only one of many functions suggested by Pareto himself; it may thus be more accurately described as a 'Pareto type I' distribution – see Quandt (1966), Hayakawa (1951). Champernowne (1952) provides a functional form which is close to the Pareto in the upper tail and which fits income distributions quite well; some technical details on this are discussed in Harrison (1974), with empirical evidence in Thatcher (1968). Other suggestions are the Beta-distribution – (Thurow , 1970), the Gamma-distribution (Salem and Mount, 1974), the sech^2-distribution, which is a special case of Champernowne's (1952) distribution (Fisk, 1961), and the Yule distribution (Simon, 1955, Simon and Bonini, 1958). Hastings and Peacock (1974) provide a very useful summary of the mathematical properties of many of the above.

175

CHAPTER 5

Notes. If you want a fuller introduction to the problem of
specifying an income or wealth variable, see Atkinson
(1975). The quality of the data, of course, depends
crucially on the type of tax administration and official
statistical service for the country in question. On the
one hand extremely comprehensive and detailed information
about income and wealth (including cross-classifications
of these two) is provided, for example, by the Swedish
Central Statistical Bureau, on the basis of tax returns.
On the other, one must overcome almost insuperable
difficulties where the data presentation is messy,
incomplete or designedly misleading. An excellent example
of the effort required here is provided by the geometric
detective work of Wiles and Markowski (1971) and Wiles
(1974) in handling Soviet earnings distribution data.
Fortunately for the research worker, some government
statistical services, such as the UK's Central Statistical
Office, modify the raw tax data so as to improve the concept
of income and to represent low incomes more satisfactorily.
Stark (1972) gives a detailed account of the significance
of refinements in the concepts of income using the UK data;
for an exhaustive description of these data and their
compilation see Stark (forthcoming) and for a quick
summary, Royal Commission on the Distribution of Income and
Wealth (1975, Appendices F and H). For detail on income
data in the USA, and the quality of sample surveys in
particular see Budd and Radner (1975) and the references
therein, and Ferber *et al* (1969). Wealth data in the UK are
considered in detail in Atkinson and Harrison (forthcoming).

Several writers have tried to combine theoretical
sophistication with empirical ingenuity to extend income
beyond the conventional definition. Notable among these are
Weisbrod and Hansen's (1968) income-cum-wealth analysis,
and the discussion by Morgan *et al* (1962) of the inclusion
of the value of leisure time as an income component. In this
latter reference and in Morgan (1962) the effect of family
grouping on measured inequality is considered; Prest and
Stark (1967) do this for the UK. For a fuller discussion of
making allowance for income sharing within families and the
resulting problem of constructing 'adult equivalence' scales,
consult Abel-Smith and Bagley (1970). The fact that averaging
incomes over longer periods reduces the resulting inequality
statistics emerges convincingly from the work of Hanna *et al*
(1948). The key reference on the theoretical and empirical
importance of price changes on measured inequality is

Muellbauer (1974). A further complication which needs to be noted from Metcalf (1969) is that the way in which price changes affect low-income households may depend on household composition; whether there is a male bread-winner present is particularly important. International comparisons of inequality within countries are found in Paukert (1973) and Jain (1975), though neither discusses fully the problems of international comparison of data, which is done in Kuznets (1963, 1966). Beckerman and Bacon (1970) provide a novel approach to the measurement of world (i.e. inter-country) inequality by constructing their own index of 'income per head' for each country from the consumption of certain key commodities.

Several large comprehensive datasets of individual incomes exist. A good description of one such dataset from the USA Internal Revenue Service and Survey of Economic Opportunity figures for some 72,000 families and single people is provided by Okner (1972); for the quantitative significance in terms of measured inequality of the different definitions of income which this data-file approach permits, consult Okner (1975).

If you are working with data presented in the conventional grouped form, then the key reference on the computation of the bounds J_L, J_U is Gastwirth (1975). Now in addition to the bounds on inequality measures that we considered in the text Gastwirth shows that if one may assume 'decreasing density' over a particular income interval (i.e. the frequency curve is sloping downwards to the right in the given income bracket) then one can calculate bounds J'_L, J'_U that are much sharper – i.e. the bounds J'_L, J'_U lie *within* the range of inequality values (J_L, J_U) which we computed. The use of these refined bounds leaves the qualitative conclusions of pages 132-134 unchanged, though the proportional gap is reduced a little. The special case of the Gini index is treated in Gastwirth (1972), Mehran (1975) shows that you can work out bounds on G simply from a set of sample observations on the Lorenz curve without having to know either mean income $\bar{y}$ or the class limits $a_1, a_2, \ldots a_{k+1}$. In the two Gastwirth references there are also some refined procedures for taking into account the open-ended interval forming the top income bracket – an awkward problem if the total amount of income in this interval is unknown. As an alternative to the methods discussed in the appendix (using the Pareto interpolation, or fitting Paretian density functions), the procedure for interpolating on Lorenz curves introduced by Gastwirth and Glauberman (1976) works quite well.

The standard error for the coefficient of variation is taken from Weatherburn (1949, p. 144) for Gini's mean difference (related to the Gini coefficient of concentration) from Kendall and Stuart (1958) and from David (1968), for the relative mean deviation from Gastwirth (1974), and for the variance of logarithms of incomes from Aitchison and Brown (1959, p. 39). For information on the concept of the standard error see Kendall and Stuart or (fairly easy) Reichmann (1961).

If you want to estimate lognormal curves from grouped or ungrouped data, you should refer to Aitchison and Brown (1959, pp. 38-43, 51-54) first. Quandt (1966) deals with the estimation of Pareto's α for ungrouped data. Now the ordinary least squares method, discussed by Quandt, despite its simplicity has some undesirable statistical properties, as explained in Aigner and Goldberger (1970). In the latter paper you will find a discussion of the difficult problem of providing maximum likelihood estimates for α from grouped data. The fact that in estimating a Pareto curve a fit is made to cumulative series which may provide a misleadingly good fit was noted in Johnson (1937), while Champernowne (1956) provided the warning about uncritical use of the correlation coefficient as a criterion of suitability of fit. The suggestion of using inequality measures as an alternative basis for testing goodness-of-fit was first put forward by Gastwirth and Smith (1972), where they test the hypothesis of lognormality for United States IRS data. To test for lognormality one may examine whether the skewness and the kurtosis ('peakedness') of the observed distribution of the logarithms of incomes are significantly different from those of a normal distribution; for details consult Kendall and Stuart.

The formulas in the appendix for the decomposition of inequality measures are standard. One obvious omission is the Gini index, the decomposition of which presents serious problems of interpretation. However Pyatt (1976) tackles this by decomposing the Gini index into a component that represents within-group inequality, one that gives between-group inequality, and one that depends on the extent to which income distributions in different groups overlap one another.

References

Abel-Smith, B. and Bagley, C. (1970), 'The problem of
    establishing equivalent standards of living for families
    of different composition', *in* Townsend, P. (ed), *The
    Concept of Poverty*, Heinemann, London.
Adams, K. (1976), 'Pareto's answer to inflation', *New
    Scientist*, *71*, 534-537.
Addo, H. (1976), 'Trends in international value-inequality
    1969-1970: an empirical study', *Journal of Peace
    Research*, *13*, 13-34.
Aigner, D. J. and Goldberger, A. S. (1970), 'Estimation of
    Pareto's Law from grouped observations', *Journal of
    the American Statistical Association*, *65*, 712-723.
Aigner, D. J. and Heins, A. J. (1967), 'A social welfare
    view of the measurement of income inequality', *Review
    of Income and Wealth*, *13*, 175-184.
Aitchison, J. and Brown, J. A. C. (1954), 'On criteria for
    descriptions of income distribution', *Metroeconomica*,
    6, 88-107.
Aitchison, J. and Brown, J. A. C. (1957), *The Lognormal
    Distribution*, Cambridge University, Press, London.
Alker, H. R., Jr. (1965), *Mathematics and Politics*,
    Macmillan, New York.
Alker, H. R., Jr. and Russet, B. (1964), 'On measuring
    inequality', *Behavioral Science*, *9*, 207-218.

Allen, R. G. D. (1949), *Statistics for Economists*, Hutchinson, London.

Arrow, K. J. (1973), 'Some ordinalist-utilitarian notes on Rawls' theory of justice', *Journal of Philosophy*, 70, 245-263.

Atkinson, A. B. (1970), 'On the measurement of inequality', *Journal of Economic Theory*, 2, 244-263. Reprinted with nontechnical addendum in Atkinson (1973).

Atkinson, A. B. (1973), *Wealth, Income and Inequality*, Penguin, Harmondsworth.

Atkinson, A. B. (1974), 'Poverty and income inequality in Britain', *in* Wedderburn, D. (Ed.), *Poverty, Inequality and The Class Structure*, Cambridge University Press, London.

Atkinson, A. B. (1975), *The Economics of Inequality*, Oxford University Press, London.

Atkinson, A. B. (1975a), 'The distribution of wealth in Britain in the 1960s - the estate duty method re-examined', *in* Smith, J. D. (ed.), *The Personal Distribution of Income and Wealth*, National Bureau of Economic Research, New York.

Atkinson, A. B. and Harrison, A. J. (forthcoming), *The Distribution of Personal Wealth in Britain*, Cambridge University Press, London.

Batchelder, A. B. (1971), *The Economics of Poverty*, Wiley, New York.

Beckerman, W. and Bacon, R. (1970), 'The international distribution of incomes', *in* Streeten, P. (ed.), *Unfashionable Economics. Essays in Honour of Lord Balogh*, Weidenfeld and Nicolson, London.

Bentzel, R. (1970), 'The social significance of income distribution statistics', *Review of Income and Wealth*, 16, 253-264.

Bernadelli, H. (1944), 'The stability of the income distribution', *Sankhya*, 6, 351-362.

Bjerke, K. (1970), 'An analysis of the distribution of wages in Copenhagen in the second quarter of 1951', *Review of Income and Wealth*, 16, 333-352.

Board of Inland Revenue (1972), *Survey of Personal Incomes 1969-1970*, HMSO, London.

Boulding, K. E. (1975), 'The pursuit of equality', *in* Smith, J. D. (ed.), *The Personal Distribution of Income and Wealth*, National Bureau of Economic Research, New York.

Bowen, I. (1970), *Acceptable Inequalities*, Allen and Unwin, London.

Bowman, M. J. (1945), 'A graphical analysis of personal income distribution in the United States', *American Economic Review*, *35*, 607-628.

Bronfenbrenner, M. (1971), *Income Distribution Theory*, Macmillan, London.

Brown, A. J. (1972), *The Framework of Regional Economics in The United Kingdom*, Cambridge University Press, London.

Brown, J. A. C. (1976), 'The mathematical and statistical theory of income distribution', *in* Atkinson, A. B. (ed.) *The Personal Distribution of Income and Wealth*, Allen and Unwin, London.

Budd, E. C. (1970), 'Postwar changes in the size distribution of income in the US', *American Economic Review, Papers and Proceedings*, *60*, 247-260.

Budd, E. C. and Radner, D. B. (1975), 'The Bureau of Economic Analysis and Current Population Survey size distributions: some comparisons for 1964', *in* Smith, J. D. (ed.), *The Personal Distribution of Income and Wealth*, National Bureau of Economic Research, New York.

Champernowne, D. G. (1952), 'The graduation of income distributions', *Econometrica*, *20*, 591-615.

Champernowne, D. G. (1953), 'A model of income distribution', *Economic Journal*, *63*, 318-351. Reprinted in Champernowne (1973).

Champernowne, D. G. (1956), 'Comment on the paper by P. E. Hart and S. J. Prais', *Journal of The Royal Statistical Society, A 119*, 181-183.

Champernowne, D. G. (1973), *The Distribution of Income Between Persons*, Cambridge University Press, London.

Champernowne, D. G. (1974), 'A comparison of measures of inequality of income distribution', *Economic Journal*, *84*, 787-816.

Chipman, J. S. (1974), 'The welfare ranking of Pareto distributions', *Journal of Economic Theory*, *9*, 275-282.

Connor, L. R. and Morrell, A. J. H. (1964), *Statistics in Theory and Practice*, 5th edn, Pitman, London.

Cowell, F. A. (1975), 'Income tax incidence in an ageing population. An examination of the measurement of income redistribution', *European Economic Review*, *6*, 343-367.

Cowell, F. A. and Kuga, K. (1976), 'Inequality measurement: an axiomatic approach', *University of Keele Discussion Paper*, No. 9.

Dalton, H. (1920), 'The measurement of the inequality of incomes', *Economic Journal*, *30*, 348-361.

Dasgupta, A. K. and Pearce, D. W. (1972), *Cost-Benefit Analysis*, Macmillan, London.

Dasgupta, P., Sen, A. K. and Starrett, D. (1973), 'Notes on the measurement of inequality', *Journal of Economic Theory*, *6*, 180-187.

David, H. A. (1968), 'Gini's Mean Difference rediscovered', *Biometrika*, *55*, 573-575.

Davis, H. T. (1941), *The Analysis of Economic Time Series*, Principia Press, Bloomington, Indiana.

Davis, H. T. (1954), *Political Statistics*, Principia Press, Evanston, Illinois.

Élteto, O. and Frigyes, E. (1968), 'New inequality measures as efficient tools for causal analysis and planning', *Econometrica*, *36*, 383-396.

Esberger, S. E. and Malmquist, S. (1972), *En Statistisk Studie av Inkomstutvecklingen (A Statistical Study of The Development of Incomes)*, Statistiska Centralbyrån och Bostadsstyrelsen, Stockholm.

Fase, M. M. G. (1970), *An Econometric Model of Age Income Profiles, A Statistical Analysis of Dutch Income Data 1958-1967*, Rotterdam University Press.

Ferber, R., Forsythe, J., Guthrie, H. W. and Maynes, E. S. (1969), 'Validation of a national survey of consumer financial characteristics', *Review of Economics and Statistics*, *51*, 436-444.

Fisk, P. R. (1961), 'The graduation of income distributions', *Econometrica*, *29*, 171-185.

Francis, W. L. (1972), *Formal Models of American Politics: An Introduction*, Harper and Row, New York.

Gastwirth, J. L. (1971), 'A general definition of the Lorenz curve', *Econometrica*, *39*, 1037-1039.

Gastwirth, J. L. (1972), 'The estimation of the Lorenz curve and the Gini index', *Review of Economics and Statistics*, *54*, 306-316.

Gastwirth, J. L. (1974), 'Large sample theory of some measures of income inequality', *Econometrica*, *42*, 191-196.

Gastwirth, J. L. (1975), 'The estimation of a family of measures of economic inequality', *Journal of Econometrics*, *3*, 61-70.

Gastwirth, J. L. and Glauberman, M. (1976), 'The interpolation of the Lorenz curve and Gini index from grouped data', *Econometrica*, *44*, 479-483.

Gastwirth, J. L. and Smith, J. T. (1972), 'A new goodness-of-fit test', *Proceedings of The American Statistical Association*, 320-322.

Gini, C. (1912), *Variabilità e Mutabilità*, Bologna.

Graaff, J. de V. (1957), *Theoretical Welfare Economics*, Cambridge University Press, London.

Hammond, P. J. (1975), 'A note on extreme inequality aversion', *Journal of Economic Theory*, *11*, 465-467.

Hanna, F. A., Pechman, J. A. and Lerner, S. M. (1948), *Analysis of Wisconsin Income*, National Bureau of Economic Research, New York.

Hannah, L. and Kay, J. A. (1977), *Concentration in British Industry; Theory, Measurement and the UK experience*, Macmillan, London.

Harrison, A. J. (1974), 'Inequality of income and the Champernowne distribution', *University of Essex, Department of Economics Discussion Paper*, No. 54.

Hart, P. E. and Prais, S. J. (1956), 'An analysis of business concentration', *Journal of The Royal Statistical Society, A 119*, 150-181.

Hastings, N. A. J. and Peacock, J. B. (1974), *Statistical Distributions*, Butterworths, London.

Hayakawa, M. (1951), 'The application of Pareto's law of income to Japanese data', *Econometrica*, *19*, 174-183.

Helmert, F. R. (1876), 'Die Berechnung des wahrscheinlichen Beobachtungsfehlers aus den ersten Potenzen dur Differenzen gleichgenauer direkter Beobachtungen', *Astronomische Nachrichten*, *88*, 127-132.

Herfindahl, O. C. (1950), *Concentration in the Steel Industry*, Ph.D. dissertation, Columbia University.

Hill, T. P. (1959), 'An analysis of the distribution of wages and salaries in Great Britain', *Econometrica*, *27*, 355-381.

Hoel, P. G. (1966), *Elementary Statistics*, 2nd edn, Wiley, New York.

Jain, S. (1975), *Size Distribution of Income. A Compilation of Data*, World Bank, Washington.

Jencks, C. (1973), *Inequality*, Allen Lane, London.

Johnson, N. O. (1937), 'The Pareto Law', *Review of Economic Statistics*, *19*, 20-26.

Keeping, E. S. (1962), *Introduction to Statistical Inference*, Van Nostrand Reinhold, New York.

Kendall, M. G. and Stuart, A. (1958), *The Advanced Theory of Statistics*, Griffin, London.

Kolm, S.-Ch. (1969), 'The optimal production of social justice', *in* Margolis, J. and Guitton, H. (ed), *Public Economics*, Macmillan, London.

Kolm, S.-Ch. (1976), 'Unequal inequalities', *Journal of Economic Theory*, *12*, 416-442; *13*, 82-111.

Kondor, Y. (1971), 'An old-new measure of income inequality', *Econometrica*, *39*, 1041-1042.

Kondor, Y. (1975), 'Value judgements implied by the use of various measures of income inequality', *Review of Income and Wealth*, *21*, 309-321.

183

Kuga, K. (1973), 'Measures of income inequality: an axiomatic approach', *Osaka University, Institute of Social and Economic Research Discussion Paper*, No. 76.

Kuznets, S. (1959), *Six Lectures on Economic Growth*, Free Press of Glencoe, Illinois.

Kuznets, S. (1963), 'Quantitative aspects of the economic growth of nations: part VIII, distribution of income by size', *Economic Development and Cultural Change, 11.*

Kuznets, S. (1966), *Modern Economic Growth*, Yale University Press, New Haven, Connecticut.

Lebergott, S. (1959), 'The shape of the income distribution', *American Economic Review, 49*, 328-247.

Levine, D. B. and Singer, N. M. (1970), 'The mathematical relation between the income density function and the measurement of income inequality', *Econometrica, 38*, 324-330.

Little, I. M. D. and Mirrlees, J. A. (1974), *Project Appraisal and Planning in Developing Countries*, Heinemann, London.

Lindley, D. V. and Miller, J. C. P. (1966), *Cambridge Elementary Statistical Tables*, Cambridge University Press, London.

Lorenz, M. C. (1905), 'Methods of measuring the concentration of wealth', *Publications of the American Statistical Association, 9*, 209-219.

Love, R. and Wolfson, M. C. (1976), *Income Inequality: Statistical Methodology and Canadian Illustrations*, Statistics Canada, Ottawa.

Lydall, H. F. (1959), 'The long-term trend in the size distribution of income', *Journal of the Royal Statistical Society, A 122*, 1-36.

Lydall, H. F. (1968), *The Structure of Earnings*, Oxford University Press, London.

Mandelbrot, B. (1960), 'The Pareto-Levy law and the distribution of income', *International Economic Review, 1*, 79-106.

Marfels, C. (1971), 'Einige neuere Entwicklungen in der Messung der industriellen Konzentration' ('Some new developments in the measurement of industrial concentration'), *Metrika, 17*, 753-766.

Mayston, D. J. (1974), *The Idea of Social Choice*, Macmillan, London.

Meade, J. E. (1976), *The Just Economy*, Allen and Unwin, London.

Mehran, F. (1975), 'Bounds on the Gini index based on observed points of the Lorenz curve', *Journal of the American Statistical Association, 70*, 64-66.

184

Mera, K. (1969), 'Experimental determination of relative marginal utilities', *Quarterly Journal of Economics*, *83*, 464-477.

Metcalf. C. E. (1969), 'The size distribution of personal income during the business cycle', *American Economic Review*, *59*, 657-668.

Mood, A. M. and Graybill, F. A. (1963), *Introduction to The Theory of Statistics*, McGraw-Hill, New York.

Morgan, J. N. (1962), 'The anatomy of income distribution', *Review of Economics and Statistics*, *44*, 270-283.

Morgan, J. N., David, M. H., Cohen, W. J. and Brazer, A. E. (1962), *Income and Welfare in The United States*, McGraw-Hill, New York.

Muellbauer, J. (1974), 'Prices and inequality: the United Kingdom experience', *Economic Journal*, *84*, 32-55.

Musgrave, R. A. and Thin, T. (1948), 'Income Tax Progression, 1929-48', *Journal of Political Economy*, *56*, 498-514.

Nicholson, R. J. (1969), *Economic Statistics and Economic Problems*, McGraw-Hill, London.

Okner, B. A. (1972), 'Constructing a new data base from existing microdata sets: the 1966 MERGE file', *Annals of Economic and Social Measurement*, *1*, 325-342.

Okner, B. A. (1975), 'Individual taxes and the distribution of income', *in* Smith, J. D. (ed), *The Personal Distribution of Income and Wealth*, National Bureau of Economic Research, New York.

Okun, A. M. (1975), *Equality and Efficiency, The Big Trade-off*, Brookings, Washington.

Paglin, M. (1975), 'The measurement and trend of inequality: a basic revision', *American Economic Review*, *65*, 598-609.

Pareto, V. (1965), *Écrits sur La Courbe de la Repartition de la Richesse*, (G. Busino, ed), vol. 3 of *Oeuvres Complète*, Librairie Droz, Geneva.

Pareto, V. (1972), *Manual of Political Economy*, (A. S. Schwier and A. N. Page, eds), Macmillan, London.

Paukert, F. (1973), 'Income distribution at different levels of development: a survey of the evidence', *International Labour Review*, *108*, 97-125.

Pen, J. (1974), *Income Distribution*, 2nd edn, Penguin, Harmondsworth.

Phelps, E. S. (1973), *Economic Justice*, Penguin, Harmondsworth.

Pigou, A. C. (1952), *The Economics of Welfare*, 4th edn, Macmillan, London.

Polanyi, G. and Wood, J. B. (1974), *How much Inequality?*, Institute of Economic Affairs Research Monograph, London.

Prest, A. R. and Bauer, P. T. (1973), 'Income differences and inequalities', *Moorgate and Wall Street*, Autumn, 22-43.

Prest, A. R. and Stark, T. (1967), 'Some aspects of income distribution in the UK since World War II', *Manchester School*, *35*, 217-243.

Pyatt, G. (1976), 'On the interpretation and disaggregation of Gini coefficients', *Economic Journal*, *86*, 243-255.

Quandt, R. (1966), 'Old and new methods of estimation and the Pareto distribution', *Metrika*, *10*, 55-82.

Rawls, J. (1972), *A Theory of Justice*, Oxford University Press, London.

Rees, J. (1971), *Equality*, Pall Mall, London.

Reichmann, W. J. (1961), *Use and Abuse of Statistics*, Methuen, London.

Rein, M. and Miller, S. M. (1974), 'Standards of income re-distribution', *Challenge*, July/August, 20-26.

Rosenbluth, G. (1955), 'Measures of concentration', *in* Stigler, G. J. (ed), *Business Concentration and Price Policy*, National Bureau of Economic Research, Princeton.

Royal Commission on The Distribution of Income and Wealth (1975), *Report No 1: Initial Report on The Standing Reference*, Cmnd 6171, HMSO, London.

Royal Commission on The Distribution of Income and Wealth (1976), *Report No 3: Higher Incomes From Employment*, Cmnd 6383, HMSO, London.

Royal Commission on the Taxation of Profits and Incomes (1955), *Final Report*, Cmd 9474, HMSO, London.

Russett, B. M. (1964), 'Inequality and instability: the relation of land tenure to politics', *World Politics*, *16*, 442-454.

Salem, A. B. Z. and Mount, T. D. (1974), 'A convenient descriptive model of income distribution: the gamma density', *Econometrica*, *42*, 1115-1127.

Schutz, R. R. (1951), 'On the measurement of income inequality', *American Economic Review*, *41*, 107-122.

Sen, A. K. (1970), *Collective Choice and Social Welfare*, Oliver and Boyd, Edinburgh.

Sen, A. K. (1973), *On Economic Inequality*, Oxford University Press, London.

Sen, A. K. (1974), 'Information bases of alternative welfare approaches', *Journal of Public Economics*, *3*, 387-403.

Sen, A. K. (1976), 'Poverty, an ordinal approach to measure-ment', *Econometrica*, *44*, 219-231.

Simon, H. A. (1955), 'On a class of skew distribution functions', *Biometrika*, *52*, 425-440.

Simon, H. A. (1957), 'The compensation of executives', *Sociometry*, *20*, 32-35. Reprinted in Atkinson (1973).

Simon, H. A. and Bonini, C. P. (1958), 'The size distribution of business firms', *American Economic Review*, *48*, 607-617.

Singh, S. K. and Maddala, G. S. (1976), 'A function for the
size distribution of incomes', *Econometrica*, *44*, 963-970.
Soltow, L. (1975), 'The wealth, income and social class of
men in large northern cities of the United States in
1860', *in* Smith, J. D. (ed), *The Personal Distribution
of Income and Wealth*, National Bureau of Economic
Research, New York.
Stark, T. (1972), *The Distribution of Personal Income in The
United Kingdom 1949-1963*, Cambridge University Press,
London.
Stark, T. (forthcoming), *A Survey of Personal Income Statis-
tics*, Heinemann, London.
Steindl, J. (1965), *Random Processes and The Growth of Firms*,
Griffin, London.
Takahashi, C. (1959), *Dynamic Changes of Income and Its
Distribution in Japan*, Tokyo.
Tawney, R. H. (1964), *Equality*, Allen and Unwin, London.
Extract in Atkinson (1973).
Thatcher, A. R. (1968), 'The distribution of earnings of
employees in Great Britain', *Journal of The Royal
Statistical Society*, A *131*, 133-170.
Theil, H. (1967), *Economics and Information Theory*, North
Holland, Amsterdam.
Thurow, L. C. (1970), 'Analyzing the American income
distribution', *American Economic Review*, *Papers and
Proceedings*, *60*, 261-269.
Thurow, L. C. (1975), *Generating Inequality*, Basic Books,
New York.
Tobin, J. (1970), 'On limiting the domain of inequality',
Journal of Law and Economics, *13*, 263-277. Reprinted in
Phelps (1973).
United Nations Economic Commission For Europe (1957),
Economic Survey of Europe in 1956, Geneva.
van der Wijk (1939), *Inkomens- en Vermogensverdeling*,
(*Income and Wealth Distribution*), Nederlansch Economisch
Instituut, Nr. 26, Haarlem.
Weatherburn, C. E. (1949), *A First Course in Mathematical
Statistics*, 2nd edn, Cambridge University Press, London.
Weisbrod, B. A. and Hansen, W. L. (1968), 'An income-net
worth approach to measuring economic welfare', *American
Economic Review*, *58*, 1315-1329.
Weiss, Y. (1972), 'The risk element in occupational and
educational choices', *Journal of Political Economy*, *80*,
1203-1213.
Wiles, P. J. D. (1974), *Income Distribution, East and West*,
North Holland, Amsterdam.
Wiles, P. J. D. and Markowski, S. (1971), 'Income distribut-
ion under communism and capitalism', *Soviet Studies*, *22*,

344-369, 485-511.
Wilson, J. (1966), *Equality*, Hutchinson, London.
Young, A. A. (1917), 'Do the statistics of the concentration of wealth in the United States mean what they are commonly supposed to mean?', *Journal of The American Statistical Association*, *15*, 471-484.
Yule, G. U. and Kendall, M. G. (1950), *An Introduction to The Theory of Statistics*, Griffin, London.
Zipf, G. K. (1949), *Human Behavior and the Principle of Least Effort*, Addison-Wesley, Reading, Mass.

Index

Thin, T. 87
Thurow, L.C. 168,175
Tobin, J. 169

utility function, social 43,
44,47,51,52,62,81,82

van der Wijk, J. 93-95,97,
160,164,165,174
variance 29,65,68,78,166 *see
also* logarithmic variance,
variance of logarithms
variance of logarithms 30,
31,35,65,68,84,85,131,163,
164,178
voting 106,110

wealth, definition of 4
non-taxable 111

Weatherburn, C.E. 159n,178
Weisbrod, B.A. 176
Weiss, Y. 99
welfare
index 42,46,47,48,51
weight 42,44,45,47,48
Wiles, P.J. de la F. 170,176
William the Conqueror 174,
175
Wilson, J. 169
Wolfson, M.C. 172
Wood, J.B. 170,171

Young, A.A. 170
Yule, G.U. 78

Zipf, G.K. 174